John Maeda

John Maeda
Designing the Future

Interviews and text by Chris Davis

CityU

香港城市大學出版社
City University of Hong Kong Press

Unless otherwise specified, all images in this book were provided courtesy of John Maeda.

Cover photo by Helena Price for the Techies Project.

ISBN: 978-962-937-687-1

Published by
    City University of Hong Kong Press
    Tat Chee Avenue
    Kowloon, Hong Kong
    Website: www.cityu.edu.hk/upress
    E-mail: upress@cityu.edu.hk

Printed in Hong Kong

CONTENTS

Series Preface by
Kenneth Lo

The mission of education has always been the preservation and dissemination of knowledge, a profound responsibility that our society holds dearly. Universities, often referred to as "ivory towers," are seen as the pinnacle of this mission. Yet, the scholars within these towers, engrossed in their research and exploration of knowledge, can sometimes seem distant or unapproachable to those outside academic circles. Even internationally renowned scholars are often known only as names printed on academic works, their true identities obscured by the weight of their scholarly authority.

City University of Hong Kong (CityUHK, formerly City Polytechnic of Hong Kong, which officially became a university in 1994) moved to its permanent campus on Tat Chee Avenue, Kowloon Tong in 1989. It stands in the heart of the community, fostering connections with the world. For our professors and scholars at CityUHK, imparting knowledge and inspiring the imagination and creativity of young minds is not just an academic pursuit, but a practical mission.

Scholars, despite their titles, are human beings with their own unique experiences and stories. In 2021, CityU Press initiated the Legacy Series, featuring a collection of interviews with outstanding senior CityUHK scholars and distinguished academics who have made significant contributions in their fields. This series aims to humanize these scholars, presenting their personal journeys, experiences, and educational lives to the world.

Each scholar featured in this series has a unique personality and experiences, and may have encountered hardships or faced challenges. They share a common thread—a passion for academic research and a spirit of perseverance. Though they each have their own distinct characteristics and insights, they are all committed to promoting academics. Their shared goal is to cultivate the next generation of students, embodying the spirit of "dedication and community" that is central to CityUHK's motto.

It is worth mentioning that, from the beginning, the Legacy Series has been a testament to CityUHK's commitment to teaching and learning. Supported by teaching and learning funds from the Talent and Education Development Office (TED, formerly known as the Education Development and Gateway Education Office), this series has involved CityUHK students in nearly every step of the publishing process. This includes assisting in inviting scholars, observing writers during data collection, preparing for interviews, visiting scholars, transcribing interview recordings into text, and final proofreading. This hands-on experience has added a deeper layer of meaning to the series, aligning with TED's mission to support teaching and learning, cultivate outstanding students, and inspire innovative abilities.

CityUHK fosters an open learning and research environment, encouraging scholars to develop their academic expertise and share their knowledge with students. Beyond providing the public with an understanding of academic life, I have another aspiration for the Legacy Series. I hope that young students, whether they are interested in academic research or entering a specific field, can learn from these scholars' stories. My aim is for students to feel inspired and encouraged, not intimidated or doubtful. These scholars with outstanding academic achievements are not out of reach. They have paved academic pathways, showing that with hard work and perseverance, every student can embark on a journey towards higher and further academic research.

I extend my deepest gratitude to my fellow CityUHK scholars who have shared their experiences in this series. Their outstanding research and academic careers have not only resulted in individual educational achievements, but have also significantly contributed to society. Their work leaves an indelible influence on young researchers, both today and in the future.

Whether you are a teacher or student at CityUHK, or a member of the general public, I sincerely invite you to read these stories of CityUHK scholars. As you trace their personal paths of learning and thinking, you will uncover the historical periods and places they have traversed, and the people and events they have encountered. This series is not just a record of individual life courses, but a chronicle of an entire generation.

Kenneth Kam-Wing Lo

Director, Talent and Education Development Office

Chair Professor, Department of Chemistry

City University of Hong Kong

Preface by
Paola Antonelli

John Maeda is an artist, a designer, a programmer, an author, an educator, an administrator, a producer, an impresario, and a philosopher—often all at once. His professional life has been a journey through many careers and he tackled each with courage and vision, not afraid to try disconcertingly new approaches and inject new life into ageing systems. He is a master of reinvention—of established routines as well as of himself.

With a deep passion for both theory and practice, John Maeda has left an indelible mark on the world of design not only by unveiling handsome design outcomes, but also by focusing on the elegance of the process and making it accessible to a wide audience. His lectures and publications have sparked new ideas in both the design and business worlds and his philosophy of design, which emphasizes simplicity to appreciate the complexity and beauty of everyday life, resonates deeply with a global audience.

John Maeda continues to inspire and transform by reminding us that while technology has the potential to simplify, it can just as easily complicate, and it is up to designers and citizens to keep tabs on it and make sure it remains a tool and an ally. At a time of enormous promise and wicked challenges, his critical and optimistic attitude is a creative elixir.

Paola Antonelli

Senior Curator, Architecture & Design

Director, Research & Development

The Museum of Modern Art

Preface by
Kevin Bethune

I remember vividly the first time I met Dr John Maeda, whom I will refer to here as my dear friend and mentor John. I was in San Francisco attending an MIT symposium on behalf of my former employer at the time. John was a featured keynote speaker to deliver his annual *Design in Tech Report*. When he finished, I expected to see a line of people waiting to talk with him. As fate would have it, he finished at the start of the lunch hour, and most folks rushed to get in line for food instead. John literally walked off the stage and meandered right in front of me. Nervously, I stuck out my hand to introduce myself. He allowed me the grace to collect my composure and describe my work that related to his talk. He expressed genuine intrigue, we exchanged business cards, and we met again for dinner a few months later.

Before that dinner, John was my hero that I admired from afar. Several years prior, I read *The Laws of Simplicity* which offered a peek into John's mind and worldview. The more I looked into his background (even at that time), I was fascinated that someone could weave together such an incredible polymath journey across computer science, art, design, and business. Investigating John's body of work helped me to understand that I was not alone in my multidisciplinary curiosities. Those were not easy times, when a natural curiosity to want to reach across departments to connect the dots was not necessarily welcome in most organizations. "Stay in your lane and do the job we've mapped out for you" was the typical pushback I received. Reading about John planted the seed to begin taking multidisciplinary leaps anyway.

In doing so, I learned from John that my career was mine to fully steer, and that curiosity could be my defining thread to carry me into new and exciting chapters. By watching John, I learned that every career decision never meant "forever." I could try that thing, really dig deep, deliver results, serve a team, learn a ton, and then leave that chapter for a new chapter. I would be okay. Perhaps more than okay in that I would garner unique skills, a special resilience and multidisciplinary agility to navigate complicated opportunities. That has proven to be the case thanks to John's mentorship. He also never said that it would be easy. There have been plenty of moments when I was confused, scared, or even spiraling in self doubt. John always would lend an ear and offer me a token of profound clarity that would nudge me back on course.

I was not alone in benefiting from John's counsel. In subsequent interactions with John, he opened the doors to his network of polymath friends, who all had experiences living in the fuzzy boundaries between disciplines. Often he would gather us together to find inspiration that would help us renew our sense of purpose in an exponentially changing world. John gave me the gift of his community, and showed me the power that comes from being generous by nudging doors open for others. I learned about John, the activist, the nurturer, and the "dance mom" (always cheering for his mentees and peers). It is only right that the full breadth of his story and lived experience is finally being told through this book. My hope is that other people can benefit from John's perspectives and ideas in the same way I have. Thank you, John.

Kevin Bethune

Author, *Reimagining Design: Unlocking Strategic Innovation*

Preface by
Chris Davis

With his career shaped by what he describes as a "series of fortunate occurrences," it could be said that Dr John Maeda, globally recognized artist, graphic designer, computer scientist, author, educator, and the current Vice President of Engineering, Head of Computational Design / AI Platform at Microsoft, is the ultimate all-rounder.

The son of Japanese parents who worked 18-hour days in the family-run tofu shop, from his childhood growing up in Seattle's Chinatown, Dr Maeda has maintained an unrelenting work ethic and an unquenchable thirst for learning. After graduating from the Massachusetts Institute of Technology (MIT) with his bachelor's and master's degrees in computer science and electrical engineering, Dr Maeda completed his PhD in design at the University of Tsukuba's Institute of Art and Design in Japan. He also holds an MBA from Arizona State University.

By combining his computer programming skills with his artistic abilities, Dr Maeda's early work helped to establish the groundwork for the use of interactive motion graphics that are widespread on the internet today. After becoming a tenured professor at MIT, Dr Maeda changed his career trajectory to become the president of the Rhode Island School of Design. He switched career paths again, this time to join the pioneering tech world of Silicon Valley, where he helped start-up companies to build design into their company culture. In further career pivots, Dr Maeda held senior positions with large, traditional organizations where he led teams to leverage the power of design and technologies to reimagine business strategies.

A committed advocate for inclusion and human-centric design, Dr Maeda has written six books including *How To Speak Machine: Computational Thinking for the Rest of Us, Redesigning Leadership*, and *The Laws of Simplicity* that help non-tech people to learn the principles that underpin computation and the many different ways that design is an integral, but not always an obvious part of daily life.

A noted tech visionary and sometimes provocateur for the design community, Dr Maeda's accomplishments have won him numerous awards and accolades, including the US White House's National Design Award, the Blouin Foundation's Creative Leadership Award, the AIGA Medal, the Raymond Loewy Foundation Prize, the Mainichi Design Prize, and the Tokyo Type Directors Club Prize.

Named one of the 75 most important people in the 21st century by *Esquire*, Dr Maeda is the recipient of four honorary doctorates, including an Honorary Doctor of Engineering from the City University of Hong Kong (CityUHK), conferred in recognition of his significant contributions to education and the well-being of society, core values embodied by CityUHK.

Based on a series of interviews with CityUHK, as well as research into Dr Maeda's significant online presence, by exploring his unique career path, this book aims to shine a spotlight on what fuels Dr

Maeda's resilience, his unrestrained curiosity, and why success means surviving a challenge and moving on to the next with renewed energy. As a committed lifelong learner, throughout his multifaceted career, when it comes to personal development, Dr Maeda has set an example for others by embracing change, learning by doing, and making time to learn.

Art, Math, and Empowering Allies

Escapism through education

When describing his education journey, Dr Maeda recounts his formative years with a generous sprinkling of nostalgia and humor. For instance, he quips that going to school was considerably easier than working in the family-owned tofu factory. He also says that attending well-resourced middle and high schools in Seattle during the 1970s and 1980s set the course for climbing the academic ladder. Continuing his academic journey at the Massachusetts Institute of Technology (MIT) where he later taught as a professor, and at the Institute of Art and Design at the University of Tsukuba, Tokyo, where he completed his PhD in design, was to a large extent driven by parental expectancies and personal curiosity, says Dr Maeda.

As a youth, home for Dr Maeda was in Seattle's Chinatown, now referred to as Seattle's Chinatown-International District or the International District, where his family owned and operated the Star Tofu Manufacturing Company. As Japanese immigrants, as Dr Maeda explains, his parents, Yoji and Elinor Maeda who had not gone to college, were pursuing the American dream. And a strategic part of realizing the dream, especially for Dr Maeda's father, was for their sons and daughter

Star Tofu Manufacturing Company owned and operated by Dr Maeda's parents

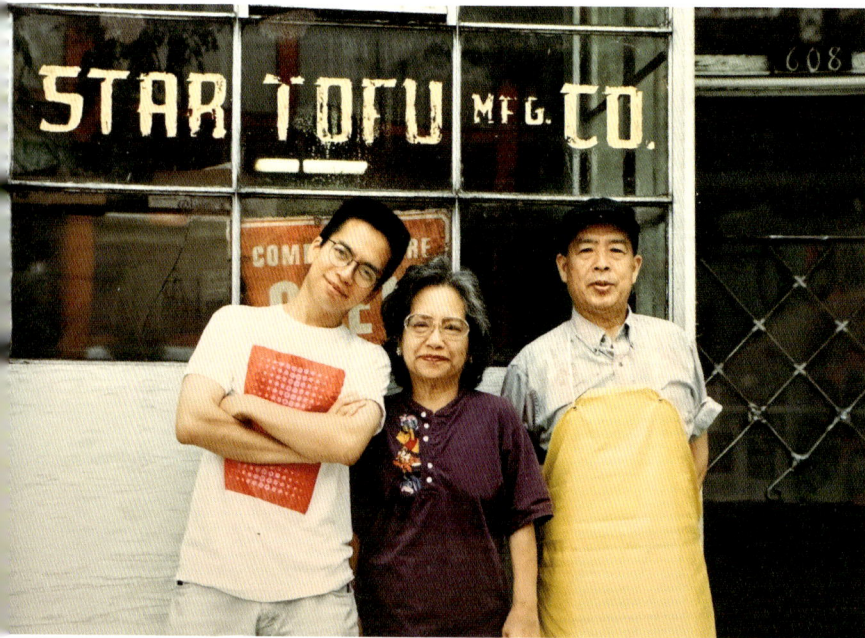

Dr Maeda with his parents in front of the family tofu factory

to study at a top-tier college which would provide them with a choice of career opportunities so they would not have to make tofu to earn a living.

The colleges of choice were preferably MIT or Harvard, the two institutions of higher learning Dr Maeda's father knew topped the tables for a prestigious education and future career preparation, even though he had little knowledge about the rigorous academics required to achieve the demanding admission standards. Furthermore, while Dr Maeda's parents understood the value of what a prestigious college education could mean, there was the pressing issue of balancing academic pursuits with the intense work of helping to run the family business.

Like many children of immigrant families, when not at school, Dr Maeda and his siblings worked in the family business, under the guidance of his hardworking artisan father. "We worked six days a week … sometimes seven," Dr Maeda recalls.

"It was intense, long hours of hard work, which some actually call 'character building'," Dr Maeda observes. "You wake up at 1am and work continuously to 6pm making the tofu."

The business sold tofu to two kinds of customers: regular people like teachers and gardeners and businesses like restaurants.

"My father believed it was unprofitable to have workers, so in the mornings we helped to make the tofu and after school we would work in the store that sold the tofu," Dr Maeda adds.

Dr Maeda (front right) with his parents and siblings

"Since we were always working, I didn't have any time to play, so school became a vacation villa; a wonderful place to escape."

While the young John Maeda may have found working in the family tofu business arduous, from an early age the experience instilled in him a lifelong respect for simplicity coupled with quality and function.

"You make something that someone wants to eat, they eat it which makes them happy, and they come back for more," he notes.

Another learning experience that emerged from working in the family business was the impact that design can have on a brand or product. In this case it was his mother's arrangement of tofu cooking photographs she creatively displayed at the front of the store, which often led to people mistaking the tofu factory for a restaurant.[1]

Favorable circumstances

Located in the affluent northern part of Seattle, the R. H. Thomson Junior High where Dr Maeda enjoyed studying in the 1970s was a 40-minute cross-town bus journey from the neighborhood where he lived with its under-resourced schools. Later he transferred to Franklin High School, which had computers, and that was where Dr Maeda's nascent relationship with computation began.

The circumstances that led to Dr Maeda being able to study at Franklin High School, which had better resources than the schools in his own neighborhood, can be attributed to one of the many "random" but fortunate "occurrences" Dr Maeda acknowledges he has benefited from. In this case a major effort in the 1950s and 1960s by the American civil rights movement that ultimately led to a Supreme Court ruling that brought about the desegregation of public schools across the United States.[2] For the first time, white, black, and Asian children as well as children of other ethnicities were able to attend school together. Responding to the Supreme Court ruling, Seattle Public Schools launched a program that would allow parents to voluntarily send their children to schools outside of their neighborhood. As steadfast believers that education could break down the walls that lead to success, Dr Maeda's parents were keen to leverage every opportunity that would provide their children with an education that would help them to achieve the American dream. And in fact, their dream was realized with each of their four children receiving a college education.

Dr Maeda has neither forgotten the circumstances nor the outcome of what studying at a well-resourced school enabled him to achieve. He often refers to his educational journey as winning a "golden education lottery ticket." Although he was only one-and-a-half years old when Dr Martin Luther King, Jr— a leading member of the American civil rights movement—was assassinated on April 4, 1968, in Memphis, Tennessee, when speaking about his early education, Dr Maeda credits Dr King for laying the stepping stones for his early educational pathway by pushing for the desegregation of public schools. In a speech Dr Maeda gave in 2009 to commemorate Martin Luther King, Jr Day at the Ebenezer Baptist Church in Providence, Rhode Island[3] (which shares its name with the Ebenezer Baptist Church in Atlanta, Georgia, where Dr King was a co-pastor with his father),[4] he told the audience how he found it pleasingly fitting that Seattle's Empire Way, the longest stretch of road he traveled along on his daily commute to school, was later renamed as Martin Luther King Jr Way.

Seattle at a time of change

Known as the Emerald City because it is green all year round, even in the winter due to the evergreen trees surrounding the city, Seattle today is a very different place than it was when Dr Maeda was a high school student. These days Seattle is the global headquarters of tech giants Amazon and Microsoft, the latter of which was founded by native sons of Seattle, Bill Gates and Paul Allen. The city is also host to a vibrant community of tech companies, many of which have relocated from Silicon Valley.

In the early 1970s, however, Seattle's major employer was the Boeing aircraft company, which at the time was facing severe turbulence caused by a devastating recession which resulted in thousands of jobs losses, and even saw the company teetering on the verge of bankruptcy.[5] The gloomy economic sentiment Seattle was experiencing was famously satirized in April 1971 by a billboard erected by real estate agents Bob McDonald and Jim Youngren, located near Seattle-Tacoma International Airport, which read: "Will the last person leaving Seattle—Turn out the lights." It was one of the first signs seen by visitors arriving in Seattle. However, the 1970s was a decade in which nothing in Seattle stayed the same.

As Seattle's federally funded economic recovery program moved into full swing in the 1970s, the goal was to build a stable economy. This meant developing an economy that was no longer anchored to the fortunes of a single company such as Boeing. Looking beyond the city's boundaries, Seattle was at the forefront of a resumption of trade relations with China, encapsulated in 1979 when China's senior leader, Deng Xiaoping, made a visit to the city, which included a tour of the Boeing 747 plant.[6]

Seattle was also in the nascent stages of laying the foundations for a cachet that would become known worldwide thanks in part to the city's coffee culture. Although it would be more than a decade before one of today's most internationally recognizable coffee brands would serve its first caffé latte, cappuccino, or Confetti Cookie Coffee Frappuccino, established in 1971, from its outlet on the cobblestone streets of Seattle's historic Pike Place Market, Starbucks began selling coffee beans and coffee making equipment.[7]

Diverse influences

While Dr Maeda excelled at school, working long hours in the family tofu business meant he was unable to take part in the extracurricular activities and courses that would help him to achieve the necessary grades to secure a place at a top-tier college. It was against this backdrop that Dr Maeda, a somewhat reserved but academically gifted student, recalls a school parent-teacher meeting where a teacher pointed out to his father how his son excelled at math and art; accomplishments his father was justifiably proud of, although when talking to friends and customers at the tofu store about his son's academic abilities, his father tended to focus on his son's math capabilities but less so his art proficiency.

"I was like, what's wrong with the art thing? I often think about that," Dr Maeda says.

While it puzzled him why his father did not recognize his art abilities, in retrospect he came to realize how his father, as a very pragmatic person, viewed math as a practical subject and a foundation for a successful future, while art lacked any obvious links to commerce. "My parents felt that being good at art wouldn't get you a good job."

Away from school Dr Maeda's main source of information came from comic books and his mom's weekly entertainment magazines, including the *National Enquirer*, a tabloid publication closely associated with sensational headlines, high-profile celebrity stories, and controversial political scandals.

"We had very few books at home because, one, my parents were not academically inclined and two, we simply couldn't afford them," Dr Maeda explains. "However, I did become an expert on Elvis Presley and popular television programs."

While reading comics might seem to demonstrate a lack of knowledge development in an academic context, as Dr Maeda later discovered, many of the story lines that fascinated him were in fact adaptations taken from historic events. "The storytellers were borrowing from Greek and Roman classical history, so perhaps what I was reading was not entirely inconsequential," he notes.

During Dr Maeda's formative years, an early source of inspiration was the original *Star Trek*, which debuted on American TV in 1966, the same year he was born. In particular, one character stood out: Scotty, the starship *Enterprise's* chief engineer "miracle worker," who processed the capabilities to devise unconventional, but effective solutions to ominous problems.

"I didn't know anything about engineering, but Scotty was one of the reasons I went to MIT to study and become an engineer," reveals Dr Maeda, who remains an ardent *Star Trek* fan or Trekkie. Staying with the sci-fi theme, Dr Maeda is known to lightheartedly refer to management and administration teams as "Jedi councils" or Jedi hierarchy, terms borrowed from the internationally successful *Star Wars* franchise.

Star Trek was also responsible for another of Dr Maeda's revelations, one with a deep social connection. At a time when it was rare to see Asian characters on television that were not portrayed as negative stereotypes, George Takei, a Japanese-American actor who played the fictional character Lieutenant Hikaru Sulu in *Star Trek*, was represented in a way that demonstrated what inclusivity and the ability to connect and unite really means.

"For the first time I saw an Asian man on TV speaking the same way as I spoke instead of the stereotyped Hollywood way that Asians in movies tended to be portrayed," Dr Maeda recollects.

This was the first time he had seen a TV series where Asian people were an integral part of a diverse community. As an Asian American and someone who tended to try to hide to fit in, Dr Maeda began to realize the value of sharing differences among cultures. This became prominent in later years, especially as his career progressed. Whether it was to bridge art and math, design and technology, creativity and business, or Asian and Western sensibilities, Dr Maeda associated the outcomes with his upbringing as an Asian American— someone who feels comfortable as the bridge that connects different entities together through his actions and existence.

Half a century after he became a fan of *Star Trek*, Dr Maeda had cause to reflect on the way that social norms had changed. Excited to attend a 50th anniversary *Star Trek* event at the National Air and Space Museum in Washington, D.C., Dr Maeda photoshopped himself into a picture of the entire *Star Trek* crew on the bridge of the USS *Enterprise*. Showing the freshly edited photo on his iPhone to his 10-year-old daughter, she, knowing nothing about *Star Trek*, enquired, "Is that Dr Mae Jemison? We just studied her in school."

In a case of mistaken identity, Dr Maeda's daughter was referring to Nichelle Nichols, one of the first black women to

*Dr Maeda (far left) photoshopped into a scene from **Star Trek** with the crew on the bridge of the USS **Enterprise***

feature in a major television series who played Lieutenant Nyota Uhura, a communication officer on the USS *Enterprise*. Dr Mae Carol Jemison, American engineer, physician, and NASA astronaut, became the first African American woman to travel in space in 1992 as a crew member onboard the Space Shuttle *Endeavour*. The moment struck Dr Maeda for being the reverse of when he was a child who thought that the character Lieutenant Hikaru Sulu was talking weirdly—for speaking normally. For Dr Maeda's daughter, for there not to be an African American astronaut like Dr Jemison in the photo, it would have seemed weird.[8]

Making the grade

While Star Trek is forever associated with the lines "to explore strange new worlds" and "to boldly go where no man has gone before," in his more earth-bound Seattle environment, as a 16-year-old student the young John Maeda was about to expand his own educational frontiers, albeit with help from his chemistry teacher Tom Wakefield, who Dr Maeda still respectfully calls Mr Wakefield. Recognizing the academic potential his 11th grade student exhibited, Mr Wakefield took the initiative to contact Dr Maeda's parents to offer advice on the extracurricular studies their son would need to undertake if he was to stand a chance of securing a place at a premier college such as MIT.

"Mr Wakefield turned up at the tofu store one weekend and explained to my dad what I needed to do if I was going to make it to MIT," Dr Maeda recalls.

"He didn't need to do that for me," he adds, pointing out how the good-intentioned intervention is one of many examples of acts of kindness by "empowering allies" that Dr Maeda credits with making a positive impact on his life. "It brings out the better angel in you and makes you want to pay it forward for others."

As his academic and career pathway progressed, it is one of Dr Maeda's regrets that he did not stay in touch with Mr Wakefield. "By the time I looked up his details several years later to get in contact, unfortunately, Mr Wakefield had passed away."

Heeding their son's chemistry teacher's advice, Dr Maeda's parents ensured he enrolled in courses such as calculus, physics, and biochemistry which would help to obtain the grades he needed to secure a place at a topflight US college. As a lifelong, self-confirmed "non-sporting" person, Dr Maeda's extracurricular courses solely focused on academic pursuits. His hard work and commitment to his academic studies paid off when in 1984 he was offered a highly coveted place at MIT to study electrical engineering and computer science. Importantly, by securing a place at MIT, Dr Maeda had helped to fulfill part of his parents' pursuit of the American dream.

Being accepted by MIT as an undergraduate student is no small feat. Viewed as one of the most academically demanding learning institutions in the world, every year MIT receives thousands of applications, but only a small percentage of students earn a seat in an upcoming class. Other than hard work, there is no foolproof formula that students can tap into to gain admission. Most notably, students must strive to maintain a stipulated grade point average, while challenging themselves by taking an array of extracurriculars and academically challenging classes. With a reputation that has become a byword for technical innovation and a pace of learning that has been likened to "drinking from a fire-hose," Dr Maeda was about to discover that studying at MIT was like "bootcamp" for the brain.[9]

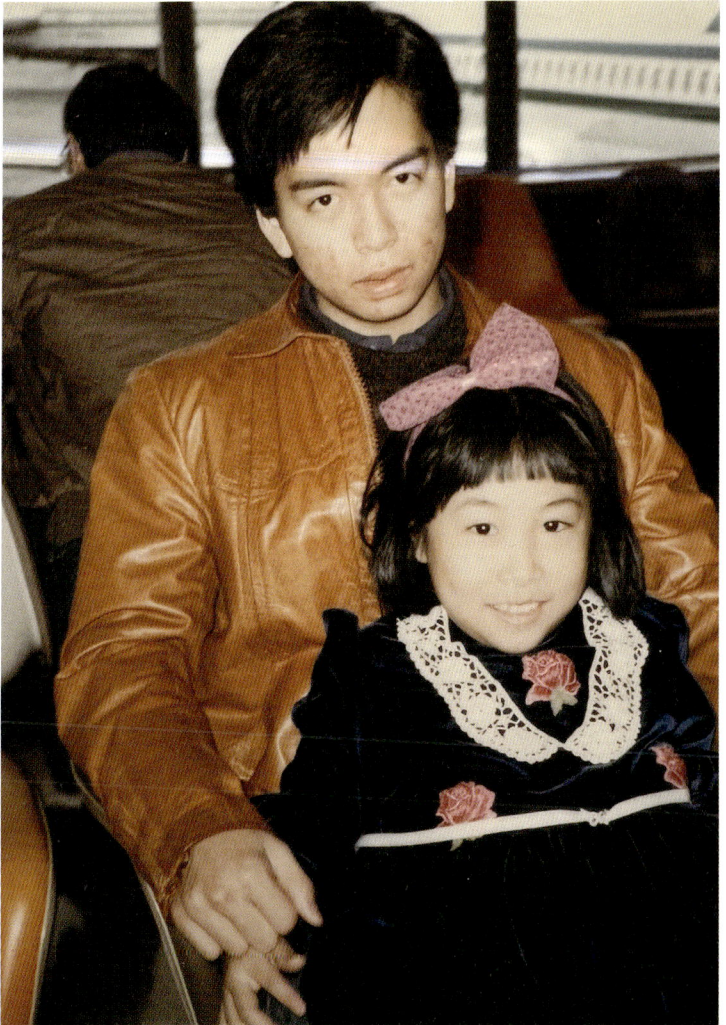

Dr Maeda with his sister Diane before he left Seattle for MIT

Studying at MIT

Arriving as an undergraduate at the expansive MIT campus in 1984, which stretches for more than a mile (1.6 km) along the Charles River in Cambridge, Massachusetts, Dr Maeda found it was more than the transition from the west coast to the east coast that took him outside of his comfort zone.

"I found myself surrounded by all these amazing people who had read books I had never heard of and had family connections with firms like IBM," Dr Maeda recalls.

As the first member of his family to attend university, there were no paths to follow, and he felt he was entering a world of uncertainty. "Here I was coming from a tofu factory in Seattle. I was confused by so many things," he explains.

Before the term became commonly used, he felt a sense of "imposter syndrome." His response to this feeling was to keep as low a profile as possible and immerse himself in his studies.

While Dr Maeda initially had aspirations to study architecture, instead, as the respectful son of a practical-minded father, he opted to study computer science and electrical engineering—considered at the time as two of the most challenging majors offered by MIT. As a pragmatic man who grew up poor, Dr Maeda's father rationalized that a career as an architect could be uncertain and might not provide sufficient income to support his son's future needs, including raising and supporting a family.

Partway through his freshman year, Dr Maeda had cause to question his choice of major, when his professor-advisor (a professor nominated by the department to advise a student on courses to be taken and other academic matters) predicted that his first term grades would at best be second tier. Ironically, several years later when Dr Maeda returned to MIT as a member of the faculty, the same professor became a colleague. Reminded by Dr Maeda how he had given him a low prediction for his academic performance, instead of acknowledging his miscalculation, the professor took credit for motivating Dr Maeda to work harder to achieve better grades.

As the end of his freshman year approached, Dr Maeda faced another challenge: how to secure a much-needed summer internship. Lacking the personal and family connections with organizations that many of his fellow students had, he sent application letters to numerous companies. With low expectations for his success, it came as a surprise when he received an offer from RadioShack in the Dallas-Fort Worth area.[10] Owned by the Tandy Corporation which produced computers that were often grouped with brand leaders such as IBM and Apple, for tech geeks in the 1980s, RadioShack was known as the "Technology Store."[11]

Once again, the job offer from RadioShack evolved into one of the "fortunate occurrences" that have played a contributing role in shaping Dr Maeda's life. Arriving for his first day at work, while introducing him to his colleagues for the summer, the vice president of RadioShack mistakenly said that Dr Maeda was a junior at MIT. The vice president even urged the staff to make Dr Maeda feel welcome so that when he graduated from MIT he might consider joining the company.

"I thought the VP had simply made a mix up," Dr Maeda says.

Thinking little more about what had been said, for the next two months he buckled down to the work he had been assigned, which mainly involved using the recently released beta form of Microsoft Windows.

The work went well, Dr Maeda remembers. "I felt I was making an impact," he recalls.

However, this changed following another conversation with the vice president when it became evident that the vice president believed he had hired a junior from MIT, but in fact he had hired a freshman. Sensing it was pointless trying to explain that he had not deliberately misled anyone, and the confusion was of the vice president's own making, Dr Maeda completed the remainder of his summer internship, aware that a future career with RadioShack was extremely unlikely. The outcome, however, was a positive one. Once able to include two months of work experience at RadioShack on his CV, the following year Dr Maeda found that securing a summer job was relatively easy.

Another life lesson Dr Maeda learned while working at RadioShack was to always check the location and availability of transport between where you are going to live and work. With little money to spare, Dr Maeda decided living out of town was a prudent way to control expenses. And with limited public transport available, riding a bicycle to and from work would help to reduce expenses further. However, he failed to factor in the intense heat of the Texan summer, especially the toll it would take on the body when cycling 30 kilometers in 30 degree-plus temperatures.

"There were times I doubted I was going to survive," Dr Maeda recalls.[12]

Design epiphany

Back at MIT, Dr Maeda diligently worked through his classes, using his spare time to design icons for computers that were just beginning to be thought of as visual tools. On campus he found a growing demand for his computer skills designing icons and fonts. People even started to suggest that maybe he should become a graphic designer. Only Dr Maeda did not know what a graphic designer did.

"I only knew what tofu makers did," he says.

This changed dramatically when he discovered *Thoughts on Design*, a slim book in the MIT library by Paul Rand, an American graphic designer and art director known for reinventing the corporate logo and setting the benchmark for corporate branding, most notably with his designs for IBM, ABC, and UPS.

"As I flipped through his book and thought, man, he is so much better than I am at this stuff, but it also made me realize

Dr Maeda with his sister Diane on the day of his MIT graduation

that this is what I wanted to do," Dr Maeda says. "That's how I discovered the field of design."

Although he was unaware at the time, in the future, on several occasions, Dr Maeda would meet Paul Rand in person.[13]

After completing bachelor's and master's degrees in computer science and electrical engineering at MIT, in 1989, Dr Maeda moved to MIT's Media Lab to begin working towards his PhD, his reasoning being the Media Lab could help him unite his passion for art with his knowledge of technology. Founded in 1985, the research focus at the Media Lab included human adaptability, artistic creation and visualization, education and communication, and designing technology for the developing world. The Media Lab and its work was a regular feature of technology journals.[14]

While the Media Lab combined a vision of a digital future with a new style of creative invention, for Dr Maeda instead of a place of art it proved too "technocentric." He also faced another challenge, an unworkable relationship with his supervising professor. As Dr Maeda describes the situation, the mean-spirited environment discouraged him from completing his PhD.

Fortunately, having seen his son complete his engineering and computer science degrees, Dr Maeda's father said he was free to pursue his own interests. Dr Maeda was also fortunate to know Muriel Cooper, a design professor at the Media Lab, whose computational design work and inspiration as a person had a major influence on his outlook.

"The funny and brilliant Muriel Cooper was the woman who showed the world how to make the computer beautiful again," Dr Maeda says. "She was very important in my life because she was the one who advised me to leave MIT and go to art school. It's the best advice I ever got."

Heeding Professor Cooper's advice and with his father's blessing, Dr Maeda moved to Japan to study art at the classic design school at the Institute of Art and Design at the University of Tsukuba located a short distance from Tokyo. As Dr Maeda explains it, the move to Tokyo was prompted by a combination of three things: the work of Paul Rand, which had inspired him to think about a future career path; the advice from Muriel

Cooper; and equally important, his future wife Kris, who was also a student at MIT, had moved to Japan for work.[15]

New beginnings: Studying and living in Japan

While invigorated by his move to Japan in 1990 to study art at the Institute of Art and Design at the University of Tsukuba, the transition from west to east was not entirely without its challenges, one of which was Dr Maeda's inability to speak fluent Japanese. At home, while Japanese was spoken, mainly with his father, and he could understand a lot of what was being said, Dr Maeda did not acquire mastery of the language to the extent where he could speak Japanese fluently.

"I looked Japanese but I was an American, which was a problem when communicating," Dr Maeda recalls. He remembers the surprised looks he received from people who expected him to be able to speak Japanese.

In an attempt to blend in, he tried using his middle name "Takeshi" instead of John, but this only made matters more complicated as people were even more puzzled why someone with an obvious Japanese-sounding name was unable to speak the language fluently.

Over time, through necessity and practice, while his Japanese language skills improved, Dr Maeda made another important discovery. Having spent many years feeling self-conscious to the point of being embarrassed about coming from a blue-collar family, Dr Maeda found himself in a country where manual labor and traditional skills were appreciated and celebrated. In the same way his father was dedicated to his work as a tofu craftsman, cooks and noodle makers, for example, are viewed as culinary heroes. Studying conventional art, using his hands, enabled him to feel in touch with his human side as well as his technology side, Dr Maeda says. In Japan many aspects of art and design are learned through food and eating.

"It can be like having a museum of modern art in your mouth," he says. "I realized that I came from a tradition that mattered to me."[16]

Writing in *MIT Technology Review* in 1998 about his experiences at the University of Tsukuba, Dr Maeda reflected on the absence of technological devices, explaining that it was a Bauhaus-influenced arts and design school with very few computers.

"There was only one Macintosh on hand, and I was suddenly free from the daily e-mail grind," Dr Madea wrote. "The absence of high technology was very calming, as was the traditional atmosphere."

Dr Maeda also explained how he experienced a sense of gratitude for being able to think with his hands in harmony with his mind. "I had been taught to honor tradition from an early age, and so the didactic ways of art school suited me very well; I was pleased to steep myself in the graphic traditions of the Japanese masters in such arts as typography, fine printing and sculpture."[17]

However, he did not completely abandon his relationship with computers. In his free time, Dr Maeda developed his own version of Adobe Illustrator-esque software, the breakthrough technology that appeared in the 1980s that integrated the use of mathematical equations to create smooth and curved lines and shapes. After spending more than a month developing a shape that vaguely resembled a moving bird wing, Dr Maeda was ready to reveal his innovative work to a wider audience, including his professors, whose reaction was somewhat unexpected.

"Why is it moving?" inquired the professors, when Dr Maeda activated the program on a computer screen.

"Because I designed it that way," Dr Maeda explained.

"But this is very bad," the professors concurred. "When will it stop moving?"

"It won't," Dr Maeda replied.

"This is very bad; very bad indeed," the professors agreed.

Dr Maeda's professors also suggested he should use his hands to draw things, not to write computer programs. Ironically, in spite of the professors' negative response to computer-generated images, within a short timeframe moving applications such as those Dr Maeda had created were in demand as web developers and designers sought out ways to support publishing for web purposes and internet plug-ins.[18]

Cultural bridges

While Dr Maeda initially found his lack of Japanese language skills and cultural awareness could be a disadvantage, there were some unanticipated advantages. When he was introduced to established and, generally older designers and artists, he often found they came from a similar blue-collar background.

There was a sort of kinship, Dr Maeda says. "I was the son of a shopkeeper and they could relate to that."

Another bond was formed through Japanese movies. Growing up in Seattle, Dr Maeda watched the same Japanese TV series and movies his father liked, which tended to be based on Japanese traditions and culture. Often these would be watched many months or even years after they had been released. A particular favorite was the long-running TV series *Otoko wa Tsurai yo,* better known as "Tora-san," starring Kiyoshi Atsumi as a kind-hearted individual whose best intentions were often misguided or resulted in unfortunate consequences.

"We shared similar movie industry cultural references," Dr Maeda explains. Not for the first time, this led to a valuable relationship with allies and supporters. "Here I was this twenty-something kid from America and I was being invited into a special, almost secretive world of traditions and ideas."

One of these allies, who would quickly become an influential friend, was the revered master of Japanese graphic design, Ikko Tanaka, who Dr Maeda has described as the Paul Rand of Japan. The friendship was cemented when Dr Maeda joined a group of renowned architects, photographers, and designers at a traditional tea ceremony Tanaka hosted at his Tokyo home. Taught to honor tradition from an early age, the following day Dr Maeda travelled several hours from where he lived to Tanaka's home to deliver a handwritten thank you note in a folder he had designed. While the other guests had sent flowers and candies, it was the handwritten note that touched a chord with the famous graphic designer. Consequently, not only did Tanaka introduce Dr Maeda to Paul Rand, he was also invited to work on an exhibition of Tanaka's work. Tanaka also ensured that Dr Maeda was able to exhibit his own work at a prominent Tokyo gallery.

"Mr Tanaka guided me on the self to understand the action without intervening thoughts," Dr Maeda notes. "I continue to embrace this conversation throughout my life."

A decade or so after discovering Paul Rand's *Thoughts on Design*, as a result of the introduction made by Tanaka, Dr Maeda was invited to Rand's studio in Connecticut. As Dr Maeda recounts the meeting, Rand was alone due to his assistant being ill. As a result, he asked Dr Maeda to stay for the day and work on the final touches of his book *From Lascaux to Brooklyn*, which Rand completed shortly before his death in 1996.

"I can't really explain the feeling of finding someone's book which changed your entire life direction, only to find yourself in a random moment years later typing your name into one of their books," Dr Maeda says. "It's a good feeling, when you can get it."

Dr Maeda also recalls experiencing another life-affirming moment that same day in the form of an unlikely piece of advice. After making Dr Maeda a bologna sandwich, something Rand pointed out he rarely did for anyone, he told him to pay close attention to what he was about to say next. Expecting to be told something profound in a *Star Wars* Yoda-like moment, Dr Maeda was a little surprised when the famous designer advised him to make as much money as he could. The rationale being it is usually the things that you do not enjoy doing that pay the most, which in turn pay for the things you do enjoy doing, but tend not to make any money from.

When he became a professor of design at MIT, Dr Maeda hosted a lecture by Paul Rand which was at 10 in the morning, early for a lecture because students usually study late into the night and are less apt to attend early events. In spite of the early hour, the auditorium was packed beyond capacity with people from all over New England as well as students. As Dr Maeda recalls, although the lecture hall was crowded, there was complete silence as everyone's attention was completely focused on Paul Rand.

After announcing he had waited 82 years to come to this place, in an on-stage conversation with Dr Maeda, Rand offered insights based on a wealth of knowledge and experience. For example, the fundamental skill is talent. Talent is a rare commodity. It is all intuition. And you cannot teach intuition, Rand explained. He also said there is no difference between a designer and an artist. They both work with form and content. Rand advocated for "keeping it simple," being honest and completely objective about your work, but working very hard at it. Such was the extent of the lecture; the line for autographed copies of his books took more than an hour to clear. His lecture was so well received that the dean of the School of Architecture and Planning, William Mitchell, and the director of the Media Lab, Nicholas Negroponte, suggested that Rand join the faculty at the Media Lab. The process of appointing him began immediately. But, unfortunately, a few days later aged 82, Paul Rand, one of the 20th century's most influential graphic designers, passed away.[19]

Career-shaping advice

Still searching for a direction following his move from MIT to Japan, Dr Maeda says it was Professor Akira Harada of the Institute of Art and Design at the University of Tsukuba who convinced him to study for his PhD.

"Just by watching him in action, convinced me that I should go after a PhD again," he says.

Professor Harada reminded Dr Maeda of what a great professor is: someone who is curious and becomes excited when others are curious, too. But he also knew how to stay on deadline; it was a combination of being able to diverge and converge.[20]

"He was someone who strove to be as energetic and as enthusiastic as his graduate students," Dr Maeda recalled in an interview with *The Great Discontent*.

Dr Maeda also described how it was clear that Professor Harada's happiness came from his students' successes—and not from his own actions. In essence, he was being a good manager and leader—and not the typical professor who was all about him/herself. "It made me think and believe in teaching as a form of 'intellectual philanthropy.' It's about doing something good for others, without expecting anything in return."[21]

Today, Dr Maeda continues to believe the impact of such inspiration transcends good teaching, quality curriculum, or entire schools for that matter because it provides the core motivation to seek higher ideals in daily life.

"You will find great people by being earnest in your work, humble in attitude, and doing your best in all situations," he says. Regardless of whatever field it may be—design, education, economics, science—the greatest form of education occurs when you have the fortune of meeting great people.

Around the time that Dr Maeda was completing his studies at the University of Tsukuba, he received a piece of advice that would both fundamentally and successfully change his outlook and career path. Professor Kiyoshi Nishikawa, known for being a traditional-minded instructor, advised Dr Maeda to stop studying the classics and "do something young." The classics, the professor said, will never change; the time to make a significant contribution to the design of the times is now. Dr Maeda recalls, in plain language Professor Kiyoshi told him that unless he did something new he would be behaving in a manner equivalent to a horse's rear end.

Heeding the professor's advice and driven by a sense of liberation, after four years of being immersed in traditional disciplines, Dr Maeda discovered the exhilaration of a new world of possibilities. Writing in *MIT Technology Review* in 1998, Dr Maeda explained how he was amazed by the feats he was capable of. These included making lines that moved, changed color, and stretched in all directions. "I could make a million lines, duplicate them twice-fold and delete all of them in a single command stroke," he wrote.

When he was at MIT, this was a natural thing to do at the computer. However, having been away from computers in a very different environment, he had become more accustomed to a rule and pen to the extent he was bewildered by the possibilities posed by the computer. From that point, Dr Maeda went back to technology and rediscovered everything.

"I had a new sense of respect for the potential of the medium and set out to explore the expressive gamut," he said.

Exploration of the potential computers could offer led to the creation of an image of "infinity" as a series of loops that never terminate and images of self-terminating shapes of linked splines. However, Dr Maeda discovered some of his techniques such as making pictures out of small pictures, endless textures of lines, and noise-based images had already been used at Bell Labs in the 1960s.

"At first I was discouraged and considered early retirement from the field, returning to studying the classics," Dr Maeda said. After staring at work by his predecessors for hours, he realized that although the concepts employed were similar in spirit, there was considerable room for improvement.

"It was as if a visual sleight of hand had been performed, but the trick had not been perfected," he said.[22]

Until this point, he felt the computer had simply been used as a substitute for paintbrush and paper, rather than being explored as a medium in its own right. With this conclusion, Dr Maeda set out to develop himself as an artist-engineer, with the computer as his chosen vehicle for creating art.[23]

While Dr Maeda had decided to establish himself as an artist-engineer, initially, one of the people he most admired had doubts about his career choice. When Dr Maeda showed his work to Paul Rand his response was, though the work was beautiful, to question how he was ever going to make any money doing it. "I found this odd coming from a designer. In fact, I felt I was back to square one—my father's earliest advice."

However, Rand was not referring to Dr Maeda's artistic career in general, but more specifically to the reality that there was no market for the kind of work Dr Madea was creating. The point Rand was making was that nobody would buy a floppy disk or CD-ROM to look at dynamic artworks because it was too inconvenient and expensive. This was about to change with the birth of the World Wide Web and the emergence of the Java programming language. With these two developments, possessing a mixture of graphics and computational skills began to achieve commercial relevance.[24]

Expanding frontiers for artwork

In the early 1990s, Dr Maeda notes that he was able to see how by connecting an understanding of technology with an understanding of art history, it was possible to create something new. The timing was ideal. For example, in Japan at the time, commercial interest in developing the use of computers and the World Wide Web was at the early stages of being explored. Describing this period as his "productive years" as an artist and computer engineer, Dr Maeda was able to redefine the use of the computer as a medium for expression by combining expertise in software development with traditional artistic methods.

"I was combining old-style design with new-style technology, trying to find my way," Dr Maeda explains. "I did a lot of things and made different things for different people. Luckily, that worked out okay."

In the early 1990s, another mentor and ally, Naomi Enami, a pioneering multimedia producer who published CD-ROMs, entered into Dr Maeda's life, which would have a profound and long-lasting impact on his career.

"Mr Enami was a truly amazing man, gifted with a vision and strength to do anything out of the ordinary, and such a funny guy to be with. He was always so positive," says Dr Maeda, who credits his friend and mentor with helping him to become less introverted and more effusive about his work. "I learned to leverage his powerful personality."

In the 1990s, Enami published a series of Dr Maeda's early works which explored the expressive possibilities of interactive media.

To show what computation could do, Dr Maeda made five pieces on compact and floppy disks called the *Reactive Books* for Mac OS 9. Not to be confused with books in their traditional format, in the 1990s, art produced on CD-ROMs supported a wider audience than galleries alone could.[25]

He dubbed the work as less "interactive" and more "reactive"—meaning that it responded at the full speed of an organism with fluidity and an unexpected "living" character. The first CD-ROM released in 1994 was entitled *The Reactive Square*, which comprised 10 squares that responded to input from a microphone. This was followed in 1995 by *Flying Letters*, which used the mouse as input to manipulate typographic marionettes. Dr Maeda then created the series of 12 digital

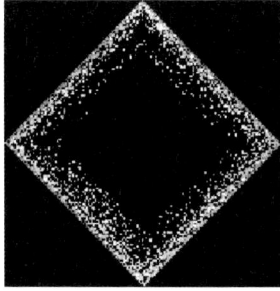

The Reactive Square (1994)

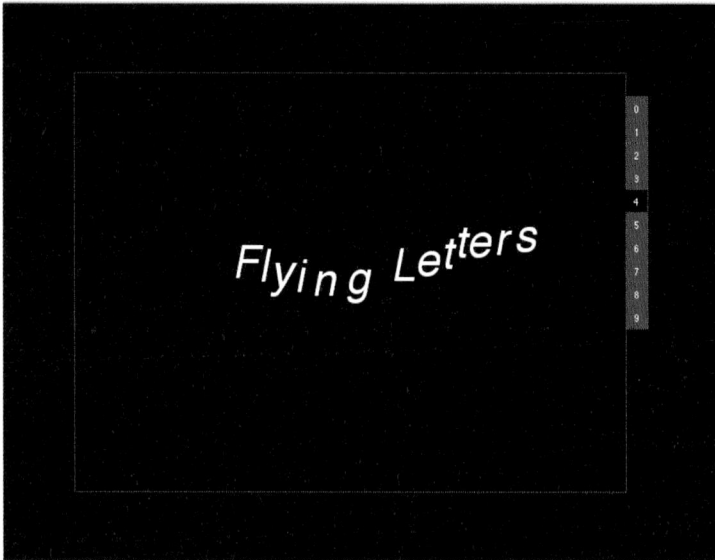

Flying Letters (1995)

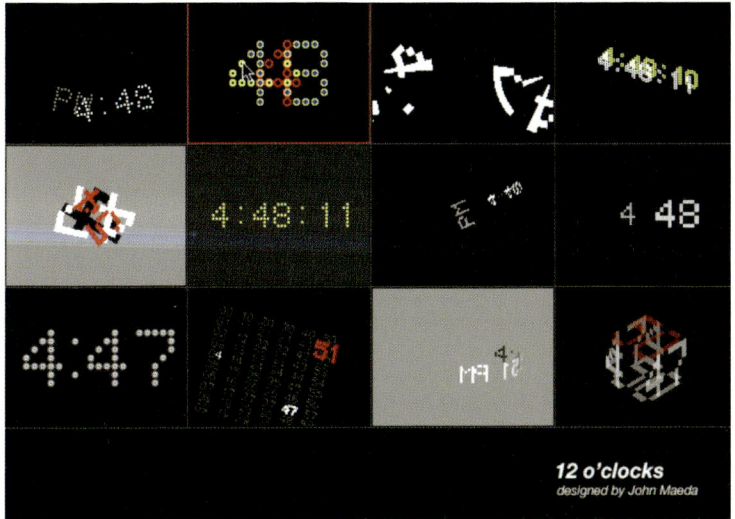

12 o'clocks (1996)

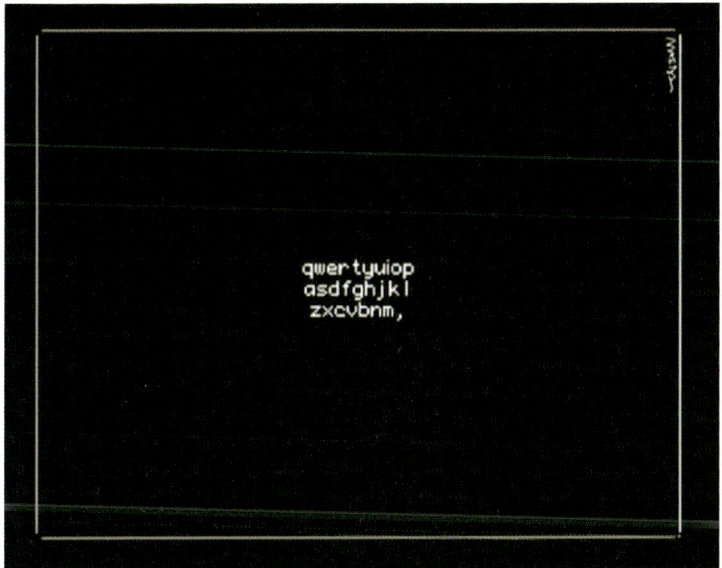

Tap, Type, Write (1998)

clocks in 1996 entitled *12 o'clocks* that played upon simple graphical time-based behaviors. Another creation in the series was *Tap, Type, Write*, which pays homage to the typewriter, stimulating playful interactions between the keyboard, the computer, and the user.

Tap, Type, Write was awarded the 1999 I.D. Magazine Gold Prize and the 1999 New York ADC New Media Gold Award. The interactive *Tap, Type, Write* was also nominated for the 1999 Milia d'Or in the general culture category. Dr Maeda recollects being in Cannes, France for the award ceremony with his eldest daughter, who was about seven years old at the time, and Enami.

"It was a big deal; it attracted lots of media interest. There was even a Cirque du Soleil performance as part of the awards performance."

Dr Maeda recalls that Enami had high hopes they would win. However, this was not to be the case. Dr Maeda remembers how the visit to Cannes took place around the time the film *A Bug's Life* was released. He also remembers the fax his daughter sent to her mom who was unable to attend the awards ceremony. In the pre-texting era, his daughter's fax read, "Dear Mom, we ate a Bugs Life Happy Meal, we watched some acrobats and daddy lost." It put things into perspective, Dr Maeda notes. Until several years later, *Tap, Type, Write* would be the last work in that particular period of Dr Maeda's interactive genre creations.[26]

Despite their lack of commercial success, the *Reactive Books* later joined the permanent collection of the Museum of Modern Art in New York and San Francisco. In a LinkedIn post he wrote in 2015,[27] Dr Maeda said at the time of the release of the series it was difficult to have them seen as anything of significance. "It was exhilarating to try to do something a bit different—a little new—and as yet undefined. But it required an early kind of 'venture capital' to get it going, and I was fortunate to have access to it via Mr Enami, who insisted that we should continue to release more of them."

Laying the groundwork for the interactive motion graphics that are taken for granted on the web today, Dr Maeda was commissioned by Sony, Seiko, Shiseido, and other companies to experiment with emerging media tools such as CD-ROMs and the possibilities of mixing design and computation via the internet. One client stepped forward before all others, an art director at Shiseido Cosmetics, Michio Iwaki. In the 1960s, Dr Maeda explains, Iwaki had experimented with computer art while he was in design school, but his fellow students made fun of him for "not being able to use a regular pen." Put off by such ridicule, Iwaki gave up mixing design and computation, but vowed to support the effort again one day. He remained true to his word.

Among the many commissioned works Dr Maeda completed for Shiseido, one that stands out in his memory is the image he created in 1995 to celebrate 30 years of commercial films. The final work is composed of a square that

Shiseido 30th anniversary poster (1995)

represents the evolution of film. With the sketches for the piece taking more than a month to develop, explaining the creative process, Dr Maeda says he did not want to create anything too tactless, and therefore used data-rich techniques in an extremely subtle way.

"I always look back to this experiment as perhaps my best work," he says.

In the 1990s, when he was writing computer code to draw things, it was not a normal thing to do. A lot of people had visual art ideas, but they could not write software to do it. For Dr Maeda, his ability to write computer code to draw moved to another level when Steve Jobs, inventor and the co-founder of Apple, left Apple to set up a new company, NeXT. Immediately after NeXT brought out a new computer, Dr Maeda bought one.

"I opened it up, started running code, and suddenly I was making stuff that no one had seen before. I was making things that changed or were ultra-complex. I was combining a deep understanding of computer science with what I had learned from my classical design training," Dr Maeda explains.[28]

Children as inspiration

While Dr Maeda has been widely recognized for combining both his computational and design skills, and developing new mediums for pushing the boundaries of art and artistic expression, less widely known is the fact that much of his early inspiration came from his children. For example, his acclaimed series of *Reactive Books* and digital pinwheels, which respond to sound and motion, were created as his young daughters sat on his lap.

"They were gifts to my children, kind of Montessori toys," Dr Maeda explains.

Many of his original pencil sketches that would be turned into animations have his two eldest daughters' writing on them. "There was a feeling of close proximity to my children," he adds. "I had time to spend with my children."

Creating computer artwork that responded to sound and motion provided a way of connecting with his children and for his children to connect with the world when they were too young to operate a mouse or a keyboard. Being ahead of his time creating interactive computer artwork did result in some amusing situations. Dr Maeda recollects visiting a computer store where his children, to the bemusement of the staff, were disappointed when they made *arrrrrragh* and *grrrrrrrra* noises at the computers and nothing happened.

"My children were saying the computers are weird, they don't do anything and the store attendant was looking at us with a 'your kids are kind of weird' expression," Dr Maeda recalls fondly.

Though they were exposed to the world of computers and technology at an early age, Dr Maeda says his children never became obsessed with computers or the digital environment. In part, Dr Maeda credits the Japanese culture of connection with the natural environment for ensuring his daughters' early education was balanced.

"Learning in Japan is tactile, so our children spent time getting their hands dirty," Dr Maeda says. As Americans, raising a family in Japan where children can walk around safely was also a good experience.

Dr Maeda's portfolio of work created in Japan culminated in an exhibition at the Ginza Graphic Gallery which took place in 1996. A total of 15 PowerBooks (a then unheard-of number) were placed alongside 50 offset-printed images to emphasize the title *John Maeda: Kami to Computer* which translates to "John Maeda: Paper and Computer" with an intended pun on the Japanese word *kami* as phonetically meaning "paper" or "god (spirit)." At the time, Dr Maeda reflects, the web was just taking off as an expressive medium, and all of his experiments in print and computing began to serve as useful blueprints for an incredibly talented younger generation.

"I could see quite clearly what was coming, and this exhibition was my attempt to put a definitive ending on my line of thinking."[29]

In 1996, after six years of living, studying, and working in Japan, Dr Maeda returned to the United States to teach at MIT, with the protracted academic title of Muriel Cooper Chair Professor of Media Arts and Sciences, Associate Professor of Design and Computation, Director of the Physical Language Workshop. It was a bittersweet moment. It was at the MIT

Media Lab where Dr Maeda first met Professor Muriel Cooper, who was one of the first graphic designers to apply her skills to the computer screen. Professor Cooper, who unexpectedly died in 1994 from a heart attack, was a leading advocate that designers should work with programming in a way that has real repercussions. Although she never learned to program computers, Professor Cooper could see the design possibilities opened up by the technology, and worked closely with programmers and engineers to experiment with new concepts in the presentation of complex information.[30]

Moving back to the United States was not an easy decision for Dr Maeda and his wife to make. As the parents of two young girls, they valued the child-friendly environment their daughters were being raised in. However, as would happen many times during his career, Dr Maeda's sense of curiosity led him and his family in a new direction.

02

Professor
at MIT

New role, familiar campus

When Dr Maeda returned to MIT where he would remain for the next 12 years (1996–2008) at the Media Lab, he was under no illusion he had "big shoes" to fill. The shoes Dr Maeda had been appointed to fill were those of Professor Muriel Cooper, designer, educator, researcher, and one of the founding faculty members of the Media Lab and head of the Visible Language Workshop. Known for her larger-than-life personality as well as being a brilliant designer and educator, Professor Cooper was recognized as a pioneer in designing and changing the landscape of electronic communication. She was also one of Dr Maeda's most valued mentors. Professor Cooper's sudden death in 1994 had left a void at the Media Lab, which was home to a close-knit community comprising faculty, students, and academic research staff.

Referred to as an "interdisciplinary creative playground,"[1] the Media Lab occupies a six-floor structure with approximately 163,000 square feet of laboratory, office, and meeting space. Together with the Wiesner Building (designed by MIT alumnus I. M. Pei), the complex serves as a showplace for new concepts in design, communications systems, and collaborative research.[2]

At the time Dr Maeda joined the Media Lab as a professor, a sampling of research accomplishments included programs that could browse databases of hundreds of thousands of images and, based on user feedback, select images using cues such as color, shape, and texture. Familiar today but groundbreaking at the time, research was also being conducted on technologies that perform tasks ranging from continuously and unobtrusively searching electronic files for references to buying or selling goods via the internet.[3]

Initially hesitant about returning to MIT after dropping out of his PhD program due to an unpleasant working relationship with his supervising professor, Dr Maeda was inspired by Professor Whitman Richards who, as principal investigator in Computer Science and Artificial Intelligence, had a vision to steer the Media Lab more towards the humanities.

In an interview published in *Eye* magazine in 2000, reflecting on what drew him back to the Media Lab, Dr Maeda explained to design educator, curator, and writer Elizabeth Resnick, "It seemed like the right thing for me." He added that the Media Lab had never been about art or design; it was always about technology. However, Professor Richards' vision that design was important to the lab resonated with his goals.[4]

Ready to share what he had learned about graphic design from the University of Tsubuka and his various experiences in Japan, Dr Maeda set up the Aesthetics + Computation Group (ACG), which brought together a community of designers who could code and engineers who could design. The ACG was intended to continue Professor Cooper's mission of exploring the intersection of design, art, and technology and her constant questioning of the processes and tools involved in the creation of new designs.

"It was an exciting time because it was the last time that academia had the edge on computing. We had the most advanced computers on the planet, and I got to recruit people who were the best in the world at knowing what to do with these things," Dr Maeda said in a December 2019 interview for *Eye on Design*.[5]

Where Professor Cooper's research focused on pushing the boundaries of graphics and information design, Dr Maeda was more interested in promoting how code could be used to create new and unseen forms. "When I was at MIT, I was in research so my job was to find new things no one had ever thought of," Dr Maeda explains.

Another of his responsibilities involved recruiting students. In his search for suitable full scholarship master's and PhD students, Dr Maeda regularly discovered that potential self-taught candidates were not eligible because they lacked the relevant college qualifications. Even though he tried to make the case for them, they were inevitably rejected, Dr Maeda says. It was another reminder how the world of academia can at times be exclusionary.

Dr Maeda's return to MIT also brought about a radical change in his family's living circumstances. In addition to three young children to look after, in keeping with an Asian tradition of children caring for their parents as they age, Dr Maeda's parents who had recently retired moved from Seattle to Lexington, Massachusetts to live with the family. Furthermore, he was under financial pressure. As well as funding his sister's college education, Dr Maeda was supporting his two brothers, who were experiencing financially challenging times.

"It was a tough time, especially for my spouse who was the person who was mainly looking after the children and my parents and doing the bookkeeping," Dr Maeda says. "It was a complex situation and I wouldn't recommend it to anyone."

As much as Dr Maeda cared for his parents, it was with some relief that, after about nine months, they decided that Massachusetts was not they place they wished to spend their retirement years and moved back to Seattle.

With high expectations of his own performance and in competition with his fellow professors, feeling the pressure to deliver, Dr Maeda would often be found in his lab with his research team working into the early hours of the morning. He also took on extra work to help to support his financial commitments. Along with his wife Kris, an engineer he met during his student days at MIT, Dr Maeda opened a design studio and ran it from his suburban living room. While at the time Dr Maeda felt he was doing everything he could to make the situation as manageable as possible, with hindsight, he notes, there was a price to pay.

"I spent less time with my children than I would have liked to," he says.

In the pursuit of success, it is difficult to find the right balance.[6]

First book

Three years after returning to MIT, in 1999, Dr Maeda published the first of six books, *Design By Numbers* (MIT Press), in which he invited readers to explore "the many possibilities afforded by creating in the raw computational medium." Using code as examples and by following prescribed simplified computer language exercises, complex forms could be generated by typing a few simple commands such as "Line" and codification of a few simple processes, such as "Repeat."[7] The intention, according to Dr Maeda, was to make programming easier for the average person.

"I wanted to broaden who could code, so I created this language called Design By Numbers. I intended to make programming easier for people who are what I call 'mathematically challenged,'" Dr Maeda explained in *Eye on Design*.[8]

In an interview with the *New York Times* in 1999, Dr Maeda said that *Design By Numbers* was "the visual equivalent of a simple bicycle" and "an attempt to demystify the technology

Design by Numbers (1999)

behind computer art, to show how simple it is, and that people can do it."[9]

Written by Italian architect, curator, author, editor, and educator Paola Antonelli, the foreword of *Design By Numbers* notes that throughout the book, Dr Maeda emphasizes the importance—and delights—of understanding the motivation behind computer programming, as well as the many wonders that emerge from a well-written program.

A review of *Design By Numbers* by Wellington J. Reiter, Associate Professor of the Practice of Architecture at MIT, described Dr Maeda's book as "a grind your own pigments" approach to programming, which has an obvious appeal to any devotee of craftsmanship and the benefits of thoroughly understanding the tools of the trade, digital or otherwise.

Design By Numbers has been credited with influencing many younger designers, including University of California, Los Angeles professor Casey Reas, a former MIT Media Lab student, who attributes his involvement in the creation of the programming language Processing to Dr Maeda's book. Developed by Reas and fellow Media Lab Aesthetics + Computation Group student Ben Fry, Processing is an open-source programming language for non-programmers who want to program images, animation, and interactions. Originally built as a domain-specific extension to Java targeted towards artists and designers, since 2001, Processing has evolved into a comprehensive design and prototyping tool used for large-scale installation work, motion graphics, and complex data visualization.

By 1999, although Dr Maeda had developed enough of a reputation for *Esquire* magazine to name him one of the 21 most important people of the 21st century, he was always willing to recognize the contribution his students made to his research work.[10]

For example, he says while *Design By Numbers* provided the starting point for the programming language Processing, as artists, it was Fry and Reas who gave the award-winning software its expressive power. Dr Maeda notes, while he is often given some credit for the development of Processing software, he almost stifled the project because he was unable to see a need for it and advised Fry and Reas their time would be better spent working on other things.[11]

"Luckily, Ben Fry and Casey Reas absolutely ignored my opinion. And good for them: the teacher, after all, isn't always right."[12]

Student centric

Throughout his tenure at MIT, focusing on what was best for his students was a constant driver for Dr Maeda, who was concerned his interactions with students could accidentally have an adverse effect on their ability to achieve their goals. With this in mind he wrote a personal "Maeda policy" he wanted to live by. The policy included, "Things that I can do myself, I either do by myself, or teach a willing undergraduate who doesn't know how to do those things by doing it for me. Things that I can't do myself, my graduate students should be doing."[13]

Elaborating on the underlying principles behind his personal "policy," Dr Maeda explains that, often when art and technology people become professors, they want to become more powerful and they will leverage their students to achieve greater personal success. A prime example would be if teachers stop making things and have their students make things for them. This can cause a culture of disillusionment. After students spend three or four years making things for the "boss," they do not want to make anything anymore, even for themselves. In worst-case scenarios, students forget why they wanted to make things in the first place.

Dr Maeda wanted to avoid this type of relationship with his students. As a result, it was, he says, part of the philosophy underpinning the activities of the Aesthetics + Computation Group, which was based on the concept that everyone in the group was independent. As such, students would work on their own projects with the credit attributed to them, not to their professors.

On reflection, Dr Maeda believes his first year as a professor at MIT was the best he could ever be. Because he did not know what the students were capable of achieving, the tasks he set them were the hardest things he would ever assign to anyone.

"They hated it," he says, and all the other professors were upset with him because the work he was assigning to students was challenging. As a consequence, other professors felt their students were spending far more time on Dr Maeda's assignments instead of their assignments.

Dr Maeda was also aware of the influence a professor could have on his or her students and the different teaching styles professors used to engage with students. In 2003, on the Media Lab website Dr Maeda wrote how he considered himself to be enormously fortunate to have had both amazing mentors as well as amazing students. "I find that as I get older my mentors all go on to the next life," but "my students improve in amazing ways. It is a mixture of the sad and happy."[14]

He also remembers an occasion that had a lasting impact on him. Walking along the Infinite Corridor that connects the east and west ends of the MIT campus, he saw Professor Patrick Henry Winston, a faculty member at MIT for almost 50 years broadly admired for the quality of his lectures, preparing lecture notes on one of the blackboards that line the corridor. Professor Winston, Dr Maeda recalls, could engage people on any subject, anytime, anywhere. Yet here he was putting work into his lectures, which were presented in a spontaneous and compelling manner.

"Wow, I thought. I should take note because I had never put that much work into my lectures."[15]

Providing a cost-effective way to present information that can be widely shared, the blackboards that line the Infinite Corridor also feature in the film *Good Will Hunting*, starring Matt Damon as an untrained math genius working as a janitor at

MIT Infinite Corridor

MIT who anonymously solves math problems written on the blackboards while performing his janitorial duties.

Early leadership lesson

In 2000 when Nicholas Negroponte decided to step away as the head of the Media Lab to pursue other endeavors, he nominated two people to replace him, one of whom was Dr Maeda. However, neither Dr Maeda nor the other nominee wanted to take on the responsibilities, while other more senior colleagues did.

"It was like a *Lord of the Rings* saga with lots of people trying to grab the power of the ring," Dr Maeda says.

As an untenured professor (it took seven years to become a fully tenured professor at MIT), there was the added pressure from fully tenured colleagues who thought they would be more suitable candidates.

"It was a humbling time because I could make things but I was horrible at leading," Dr Maeda recalls.

A particular pain point was the struggle to take charge of basic things, such as ensuring the Media Lab's toilet facilities were kept supplied. He also lacked the emotional intelligence to deal with the interpersonal demands and expectations the leadership role required.

To escape from the pressure of leadership, Dr Maeda found sanctuary in a Media Lab basement workshop where he focused on milling and polishing large blocks of plastic into artworks. Today, he still keeps an example of his plastic artwork in his office, which reminds him of the difficult time he experienced. After a year of "leading," Dr Maeda resigned.

"It was definitely a hard time, but I came out of it."

Dr Maeda adds that his first major leadership experience triggered a wakeup call that this was an area where he needed to make significant improvements, and was a driving factor that would later influence his decision to get an MBA, which he frequently describes as pursuing a "hobby."[16]

Solo book project

While committed to his work as a professor, a year after publishing his first book, Dr Maeda produced *Maeda @ Media* in 2000. With the intention of bringing to a conclusion a compendium of experiences and experimentation, it featured more than 1000 illustrations spread across 480 pages.[17]

The book provided a comprehensive overview of Dr Maeda's early digital visual artwork including computerized printouts, reactive graphics on CD-ROM, and experiments on the web. The book also focused on Dr Maeda's quest to understand the nature of the relationship between technology and creativity. The foreword, written by Nicholas Negroponte, Dr Maeda's former boss at MIT, praises the author for seeing things most people overlook, with the result that *Maeda @*

Media is a showcase for humor and expression that brings out the best in computers and art.

However, Dr Maeda saw little humor in producing his book. With no assistants to help, he found it necessary to work on the content at night, often consuming several spoons of Folgers coffee granules to stay awake. Dr Maeda explains that to keep the work on his book separate from his work as a professor required him to work through what he calls the "Batman" hours, which was mentally and physically exhausting.

"The work was literally killing me, I really wasn't well," Dr Maeda says. His determination to write and design *Maeda @ Media* without assistance, which led to him being hospitalized, was the cause of a great deal of concern for his family.

Meanwhile, recognition for Dr Maeda's contribution to the design world was growing. In 2001 he received the National Design Award for Communication Design from the Cooper Hewitt, Smithsonian Design Museum in the United States. The awards program "celebrates design as a vital humanistic tool in shaping the world, and seeks to increase national awareness of design by educating the public and promoting excellence, innovation, and lasting achievement." Praise for Dr Maeda's work included the observation, "Whether designing innovative digital calendars and game patterns or creating digital echoes of real world behaviors, Maeda exerts extraordinary control over his design process by creating his own computer code instead of simply manipulating programs off the shelf."[18]

The following year in 2002, Dr Maeda received Japan's most prestigious award for design, the Mainichi Design Prize, presented annually to individuals, groups, and organizations that produce and present significant works in the fields of architecture, fashion/textile design, product design, graphic design, interior design, lighting design, installation/ environmental design, electronic media design, and craft design.[19]

Committees at MIT

While there was good reason for Dr Maeda's family and friends to be concerned about his well-being, that did not prevent him from wanting to be involved in taking care of the well-being of others. Aware that Media Lab professors seldom joined MIT committees, as a junior professor in his early thirties, Dr Maeda was curious about the roles and responsibilities of MIT's various committees and decided it would be a good idea if he volunteered to join one. He remembers the occasion at a faculty cocktail party when he made his willingness to join a committee known to Chancellor Phillip Clay.

"He looked at me as if I was crazy, like, you want to be on a committee?" Dr Maeda recalls.

This being the era before smartphones, the Chancellor quickly entered Dr Maeda's contact details into his PalmPilot and said he would be in touch, which he was, the very next day. The committee Dr Maeda was invited to join as the co-chair was the Council on Family and Work which mainly dealt with MIT's faculty, staff, and students' family and work-related issues; a committee that few people wanted to be involved with due to the complexities of dealing with things such as child care, care for the elderly, and work-related stress.

"It was a revelation," Dr Maeda says. "That's when I began to learn how unhappy people are in a community when their basic needs aren't served."

Because of the work that was done to elevate awareness about stress-related issues experienced by staff, students, and faculty, under Dr Maeda's co-chair leadership, the committee became affectionately known as the "Burnout Committee."

In acknowledgement of his achievements as co-chair of the Council on Family and Work, a couple of years later Dr Maeda was invited to chair the Race and Culture Council, another committee that few people volunteered to join. While there was a budget available which meant that activities and lectures could be funded, Dr Maeda realized there were serious issues to address, including disparities in the way that women were treated and, whether intended or unintended, inappropriate racist language used by professors.

"I thought, wow, here we are in the 21st century and this is still happening," Dr Maeda says.

Through his interactions with students that had had upsetting experiences related to race, he became aware that people can interpret these experiences differently. Dr Maeda says he learned a lot about human nature and interpersonal relations that he otherwise would not have been familiar with.

"It depressed me, yet at the same time invigorated me with a new perspective on life," he says.

On one occasion while talking to a Native American student, Dr Maeda empathized with him and explained that as the Asian son of immigrant parents, he too had been on the receiving end of upsetting racist behavior. In reply, Dr Maeda says the student told him, "You have no idea what I've been through Professor Maeda. You've experienced immigrant racism, whereas I've experienced indigenous people racism, and it goes back centuries."

The takeaway, Dr Madea says, is that it is misguided to assume that your experiences rhyme with someone else's. "It was an awakening moment and I appreciate that young man teaching me; while I might not be able to completely relate to someone else's pain, I can learn from it."[20]

Cultivating connections with the corporate world

As part of his responsibilities at the Media Lab, Dr Maeda was in regular contact with corporate sponsors, sometimes meeting as many as three or four per day. While synonymous with "inventing the future," Dr Maeda says when collaborating with corporate sponsors he was always aware of a piece of advice that Media Lab co-founder Nicholas Negroponte gave him: "while Media Lab is smart, corporate sponsors are frequently smarter."

"That's always stuck with me, how the customer knows a lot of things, so it's important to listen to them and understand what they are saying," Dr Maeda notes.

Keeping this in mind, he says depending on which corporate sponsor he was engaging with the challenge was to find a balance between presenting them with a springboard for developing new products and ways of thinking or to continue to develop existing designs, products, and ways of thinking.

Among the useful business-related lessons he learned, Dr Maeda describes watching Nicholas Negroponte and Jerome Wiesner, who was a co-founder of the Media Lab and served as president of MIT from 1971 to 1980, bring corporate sponsors together as a "master class" in facilitating the process of networking. While Negroponte was brimming with ideas, Wiesner, who served on President John F. Kennedy and subsequently President Lyndon B. Johnson's Science Advisory Committees in the 1960s, had a broad network of connections. Dr Maeda says the combination of Wiesner and Negroponte working together was a perfect example of the young visionary holding the keys and the older visionary knowing where the doors are located.

Areas in particular where corporate sponsors were looking for solutions were the print media and the broadcasting industries. Moving towards the late 1990s, it was fast becoming apparent to the newspaper publishing and broadcasting industries how the traditional ways of operating were being disrupted by the internet. Leading the Media Lab News and Future Consortium team, Dr Maeda worked with major newspapers across the world to design and customize front-end visualization to reposition how newspapers would look and feel in the digitally driven future. What would become known as "disruptive innovations" taking place at the time intrigued Dr Maeda as being a worthwhile development to learn about and formed the basis for establishing a Simplicity Consortium to work on ways to streamline information complexity and information anxiety.

"The work was very industry focused," explains Dr Maeda, who recalls visiting corporations to demonstrate software solutions that could produce a fully customized newspaper that provided readers with personalized information aligned with their interests. "A lot of what we were doing seemed like science fiction at the time."

Instead of the standard academic theme of "publish or perish," the Media Lab's motto was "demo or die," a phrase that reflected the Lab's emphasis on rapid prototyping and experimentation as a way to drive innovation. However, the focus on creating working prototypes that enabled the people who would use them to experience them did not always fit well with Dr Maeda's fellow Media Lab researchers' who felt that writing papers or giving theoretical presentations would look better on their CVs.

The Media Lab also served as a reputable third-party validation vehicle for IT departments that were in the process of convincing their companies that investment in computers and technology was an investment in the future. If IT people could report back to their bosses that the Media Lab was using particular computers or developing a particular technology, their suggestion could sound less risky or their idea not so far-fetched, says Dr Maeda.

Nevertheless, there were times when seemingly potentially viable commercial innovations developed by the Media Lab in partnership with corporate sponsors could not guarantee success. For instance, a digital photo frame developed with Samsung, which Dr Maeda describes as being simple, elegant, and ahead of its time, was a complete nonstarter in the commercial market. In a similar way, Dr Maeda recalls, a Pinterest-like visual discovery engine developed by his Media Lab team in 2006 accumulated about 100 users, while students at MIT were talking about a new social media platform named Facebook for Mobile, which launched in April 2006 and was rapidly attracting thousands of users.

"It was an example of how ideas are one thing, execution is another thing, but timing is everything," Dr Maeda says.

At the same time, he was becoming increasingly aware that, as companies invested resources into developing technologies in-house, the efficacy of academic research, at least in the computing space, was showing signs of being eroded. The dynamics of the relationship between industry and the Media Lab had changed from a position where industry had basic or no computers to a situation where industry often had more advanced computers than those the Media Lab was using.

"In some cases we were ahead of the market, but we were also becoming too late and I noticed this," Dr Maeda says.

As corporations embraced the potential that technologies could offer, it became apparent they could scale up a lot faster than a university like MIT was capable of, even with the highest level of research capabilities. This awareness, coupled with Negroponte's insight that MIT's corporate sponsors are often smarter than the Media Lab, stimulated Dr Maeda's interest in business and leadership as well as money as a medium.

"I felt that creative people could only feel free if they were able to understand the financial underpinnings between art and commerce," Dr Maeda explains.

The revelation enabled him to realize how little he knew about the process of business and business thinking. "If I was proud of one thing at the time, it was knowing what I didn't know," he says.

As a research professor, he was one side of a coin, albeit a shiny side, nevertheless it was only one perspective. With this in mind, if he was going to develop a clearer picture of the other side of the coin, Dr Maeda decided he would need an MBA to better understand organizations and how they work.[21]

MBA expands knowledge horizons

For Dr Maeda, interactions with corporate sponsors highlighted the possibilities of connecting design, art, and technology to the commercial world, but also some of the many challenges. For example, how industry does things at scale, while in the academic world this was often not the case. Dr Maeda's interactions with businesses also highlighted a gap in his knowledge and understanding about corporate financing. For instance, he had no idea what shareholder value or customer acquisition costs related to. Having been told on a number of occasions by business professionals, "John, you're a creative guy, don't worry about the money, leave it to the finance people," Dr Maeda drew the conclusion that when enough people tell you not to worry about the money, naturally you worry about the money.

"I wondered what they were hiding from me," he says.

To better understand the language and processes of the world of business and finance, Dr Maeda decided his best option was to study for an MBA, which he did by enrolling in a part-time program offered by Arizona State University. His initial MBA experience was an introduction to a field that was previously unfamiliar to him, especially the way that money, finance, and profit featured front and center as the lifeblood of the business world.

"There were all of these different terms to describe money; money going in, money going out, and money saved, lost, and stored."

Dr Maeda says that coming from a "creative" background, for many years he had lived with an uncomfortable disconnect between making things and monetizing creativity. His MBA experience changed this. It taught him how to view the role of money more clearly and dispel the myth—which he had never believed in—that creative people need to struggle to make ends meet while people in business and finance could celebrate owning a second home.

"Having an MBA allowed me to understand how capital intersects with creativity and technology, which together unlock endless possibilities," Dr Maeda explains.

In later years when he switched his career from academia to the corporate world, his MBA-related knowledge has been useful in a variety of ways, from applying the logic of business processes to understanding the importance of supply chain management.

Applying an element of the business principles taught by MBA programs that financing is important, Dr Maeda learned that he could receive a small tuition reimbursement from MIT. However, an office administrator told him that in order to qualify for reimbursement, he would need to complete an application form and provide evidence that the program could lead to a next-level job title. Dr Maeda filled in the form indicating how the MBA program could take him from a research professor to the president of MIT.

"I wanted this guy to know that if I ever became president of MIT, I meant business," says Dr Maeda.[22]

Simplicity in an increasingly complex world

Similar to how he felt the need to better understand how capital intersects with creativity and technology, Dr Maeda's attention was drawn to exploring the benefits of simplicity. Noting how the low marginal cost of technology was amplifying the design of complex products, his inclination was to write a book on the topic.

Published in 2006 and translated into more than 14 languages, *The Laws of Simplicity*—in terms of impact and reader feedback—according to Dr Maeda, is probably the most important book he has written. Purposely limited to 100 pages to keep the book simple, through anecdotes and practical examples, *The Laws of Simplicity*, which became one of the MIT Press's all-time best-selling books, defines 10 laws for balancing simplicity and complexity in business, technology, and design.

Though it predates the emergence of smartphones that would dramatically change the way that people communicate, work, and stay entertained, in explaining his rationale for writing *The Laws of Simplicity*, Dr Maeda says he was aware that digital technology had become so complex, that even as an

MIT-trained expert in technology he found it a challenge to keep up with developments.

"I discovered how complex the topic simplicity really is, and I don't pretend to have solved the puzzle," Dr Maeda wrote in the book's introduction. He added that achieving simplicity in the digital age had become a personal mission and a focus of his research at MIT.

From 2003–2008, led by Dr Maeda, a consortium of students and sponsors including AARP (formerly known as the American Association of Retired Persons), Lego, and Toshiba at the Physical Language Workshop at MIT conducted research into simplicity through investigation and innovative approaches towards simplicity in design. During what Dr Maeda terms as his "reflective period," he started to blog about simplicity.

"I wrote as if I was talking out loud. Like most of my blogs it was a place where I shared unedited thoughts that represent my personal opinions on a topic about which I am passionate. That's how *The Laws of Simplicity* began."

At the time *The Laws of Simplicity* was published, in his review, Rob Forbes, founder of Design Within Reach wrote, "It is the most compelling one hundred pages of design writing I have read this year." He added, "If brevity is the soul of wit, simplicity is the soul of design. John Maeda uses the concept of simplicity to get at the nature of human thought and perception while drawing out tangible applications for business, technology, and life in general."

LAW 1 / REDUCE

The simplest way to achieve simplicity is through thoughtful reduction.

LAW 2 / ORGANIZE

Organization makes a system of many appear fewer.

LAW 3 / TIME

Savings in time feel like simplicity.

LAW 4 / LEARN

Knowledge makes everything simpler.

LAW 5 / DIFFERENCES

Simplicity and complexity need each other.

LAW 6 / CONTEXT

What lies in the periphery of simplicity is definitely not peripheral.

LAW 7 / EMOTION

More emotions are better than less.

LAW 8 / TRUST

In simplicity we trust.

LAW 9 / FAILURE

Some things can never be made simple.

LAW 10 / THE ONE

Simplicity is about subtracting the obvious, and adding the meaningful.

Dr Maeda's laws of simplicity summarized

Andrea Ragnetti, from the Board of Management, Royal Philips Electronics wrote, "*The Laws of Simplicity* is a clear and incisive guide for making simplicity the paramount feature of our products; it's also a road map for constructing a more meaningful world."

In his review business writer Tom Peters said, "I quickly found myself mesmerized—and thence the only issue was deciding what were the strongest words I could muster in support of *The Laws of Simplicity*. The book is important; and Maeda has made an absurdly complex subject—simplicity—

approachable and usable. Bravo! I hope the people who design the products I'll acquire in the next ten years take this book to heart."[23]

Dr Maeda credits the success of *The Laws of Simplicity*, which sparked widespread attention in the US and beyond, to "overlapping curves of interest" and "fortunate timing." The book was also designed in a way that it would appeal to the popular press, which resulted in extensive media coverage, interviews, and presentations at conferences.

The success of *The Laws of Simplicity* paved the way for Dr Maeda to suggest other authors to the MIT Press Simplicity series. Long after he left MIT and continuing until 2022, Dr Maeda introduced new authors including illustrator, animator, and professor Kyna Leski who wrote *The Storm of Creativity*. Dr Maeda was also instrumental in introducing multidisciplinary design executive, entrepreneur, and best-selling author Kevin Bethune who wrote *Reimagining Design: Unlocking Strategic Innovation* and Kat Holmes (*Mismatch: How Inclusion Shapes Design*), who was named one of *Fast Company's* "Most Creative People in Business" in 2017 and served as the Principal Director of Inclusive Design at Microsoft from 2014 to 2017.[24]

Separating academic and personal art priorities

While Dr Maeda had found success writing books, returning to MIT marked a pivotal turning point for the way he viewed and created his own artwork. Following a productive period in the

1990s when he made things on CD-ROMs, floppy disks, and the internet, Dr Maeda felt he had peaked as a "maker." Dr Maeda says he was aware of the creative abilities and the "cool things" being made by the next generation of students and professors at MIT, which made him feel it was their time to shine.

"I had had a really good run, which also enabled the careers of others," Dr Maeda explains.

While he continued to build physical objects and wrote code to stay relevant, it was not at the same level as in the mid-1990s. In his capacity as a professor at the Media Lab, Dr Maeda had also transitioned from being only a maker to a talker. "I became a 'maker-talker,' which meant I was never a hundred percent dedicated to either one."[25]

Always mindful to separate his personal work from his academic work, at various times while Dr Maeda was a professor at MIT he managed to stage exhibitions of his art. Between August and October 2001 a collection of Dr Maeda's art including *Post Digital* (2000), *Star Tofu* (1996), *Design Machines* (1994), and his book *Maeda @ Media* was exhibited at the NTT InterCommunication Center in Tokyo.[26] Further exhibitions took place in Paris between November 2005 and February 2006 at the Fondation Cartier pour l'art contemporain where Dr Maeda exhibited a system to animate a series of "motion paintings representing abstract forms in movement that recall natural phenomena" titled *The Nature & Eye'm Hungry Gallery*.[27] The following year in 2007 at the Riflemaker Gallery in London,

Dr Maeda standing next to one of his motion paintings at the Fondation Cartier pour l'art contemporain in Paris

Dr Maeda preparing for the **Media: MySpace** exhibition at the Riflemaker Gallery in London, 2007

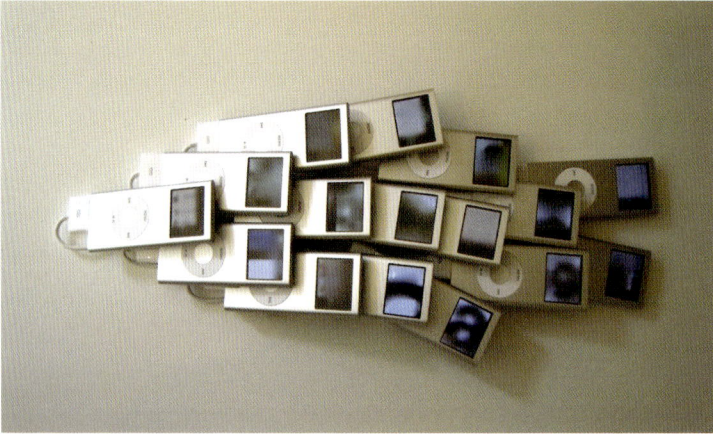

Part of the **Media: MySpace** *exhibition*

Marriage *(2009)*

visitors were able to interact with a roomful of pods, texts, and films titled *Media: MySpace* which outlined Dr Maeda's personal philosophy for achieving a "simpler" life. At his second show at the Riflemaker Gallery in 2010, titled *John Maeda is The Fortune-Cookie*, he explored how people communicate, asking visitors to choose methods of "channeling," from sending a text or tweeting to drawing in a sandbox or writing a message on the glass window with their finger in their own breath.[28]

Time for a change

After spending the best part of two decades at MIT as a student and faculty member, Dr Maeda became a fully tenured professor, which he describes as the "academia equivalent to an initial public offering on a stock market, but without the huge cash payout."[29] Still, in the same year he was recognized as one of "The 75 Most Influential People of the 21st Century" by *Esquire* magazine,[30] Dr Maeda had become restless and his thoughts were frequently turning to "what next"?

This was taking place at the same time as social, demographic, and technological changes had begun to ripple across the country, as Barack Obama campaigned to become the 44th president of the United States on a platform of change. Dr Maeda recalls how his thoughts were steered towards how he could make a difference.

Then came the call from a headhunting agency asking if he would be interested in applying for the role of president of the

Rhode Island School of Design (RISD)—one of the top private universities for art and design in the US—and in spite of some initial uncertainties, he was inspired by the feeling of what a new challenge could bring.[31]

03

From Professor
to President

Taking the lead

When Dr Maeda received the invitation in 2008 to leave his secure position as a fully tenured professor at the MIT Media Lab to become the 16th president of RISD—one of the most distinguished art schools in the United States—it was by no means an easy decision to accept.

Not having been a dean or a provost, often the normal stepping stones for a university president, Dr Maeda's initial feeling was that the offer to take on such a demanding role had arrived 10 years too early. As a professor and associate director of the MIT Media Lab, he had founded research groups and established a field spanning art and technology. As well as insights from his MBA, Dr Maeda had gained some knowledge of academic administration, but nothing he had done previously compared to overseeing a 130-year-old institution with a substantial operating budget.[1]

As an MIT professor, Dr Maeda was familiar with how a university functioned and what students expected, but as RISD president, he had stepped into largely unknown territory. With more than 2,400 students, 1,000 staff, and a sizable alumni to lead, as well as meeting budget and fundraising targets and building corporate relationships, Dr Maeda's responsibilities were not unlike those of a mayor of a small city.[2]

"I had to figure out fairly quickly what the leader's job required."

As a fully committed "maker," Dr Maeda explains that his leadership journey felt almost counter-intuitive.

"It was like I was choosing to be a leader instead of choosing to be a maker," he says, using the analogy of the professor being free to speak his mind against "the man," while the college president is "the man."

While Dr Maeda adapted to becoming a leader and the responsibilities that being the president of a leading university entailed, at the same time, as an artist, he also felt the pressing need to continue to express his creativity. Dr Maeda recalls being asked, "Do you still make your … art?" Which was said in a way he interpreted as meaning that artists make art; they do not lead organizations.

"Because I was seen as being different, people tend to doubt your capabilities when you appear in their world."

Dr Maeda explains that it took about five years before he felt he had been acknowledged for what he had brought to RISD. However, instead of feeling offended by any doubts shown, Dr Maeda says he felt emboldened.

The President's House at the Rhode Island School of Design where Dr Maeda lived during his term

"Being the president of a college, your role is to be the authoritative leader and I owned and embraced it fully, but at the same time, as an artist, I needed to express my creativity in some shape or form."

Without compromising his role as president, the solution Dr Maeda found was every day to try to make art of some type, and about once a year or whenever possible, somewhere in the world, to hold an exhibition of his artwork.

In addition to adjusting to the role of president of RISD, Dr Maeda also needed to adapt to living away from his family. With his children settled in school in Lexington, Massachusetts, close to MIT, Dr Maeda and his wife decided it would be better for them to remain in familiar surroundings.

"It was psychologically tough living away from family while doing a demanding job," says Dr Maeda as he reflects on the six years he spent living alone in the spacious President's House.[3]

Optimism and vision

In spite of any misgivings Dr Maeda may have had about becoming the president of RISD, others were full of confidence in his abilities when his appointment was announced. Roger Mandle, RISD's popular outgoing president, described Dr Maeda as "a commanding presence" and "a genius."[4] MIT's coverage of Dr Maeda's new position was similarly approving, extolling him as "visionary" and a "trailblazer."[5]

As well as being inspired by Barack Obama's campaign to become the 44th president of the United States with the slogan "yes we can" and reading his book, *The Audacity of Hope: Thoughts on Reclaiming the American Dream*, in no small part, Dr Maeda's decision to take on the challenging role of president of RISD was influenced by the dean of the School of Science at MIT, Dr Robert (Bob) Silbey.

"Bob was the person that made me believe that becoming a leader might be something I wanted to try," Dr Maeda explains.

Roger Mandle (right), outgoing president, inaugurates Dr Maeda as his successor at RISD's commencement in 2008

For three years, alongside 20 or so other faculty members, chaired by Dr Silbey, he had served on the MIT Core Curriculum Task Force, which was responsible for making high-level recommendations intended to enhance the rigor and relevance of MIT's education programs. Dr Maeda remembers how Dr Silbey had the unique ability to work calmly through the most difficult issues while effortlessly combining conviction with good humor and find agreement on a way forward with strong-willed colleagues.

"It was like the Jedi's Jedi council meeting and my absolute favorite meetings to go to because I'd get to watch Bob in action. He profoundly changed my career," Dr Maeda says. As president of RISD, he would frequently quote Dr Silbey as the epitome of a great academic and administrative leader.[6]

Wise advice

Soon after Dr Maeda became president of RISD, he received a call from his longtime friend and mentor, University of California, Los Angeles Professor Emeritus Mitsuru "Mits" Kataoka, to congratulate him on his appointment. Professor Kataoka also offered Dr Maeda a piece of advice, which he often contemplates, especially when it comes to making career decisions.

Professor Kataoka explained to Dr Maeda that life is lived in four 25-year quarters. "0 to 25 years of age is the first quarter, 25 to 50 years old is the second, 50 to 75 is the third quarter, and 75 to 100 is the fourth."

During the phone conversation, pointing out that many people do not make it to the fourth quarter and for most people the body starts to deteriorate in the third quarter—noting that Dr Maeda 41 years old at the time and well into his second quarter—Professor Kataoka strongly advised him not to waste his second quarter, and therefore "do something with yourself in this job."

Not long before Professor Kataoka passed away in 2018, Dr Maeda was able to update him on his achievements at RISD, especially in the areas of helping to link science and technology with innovation and economic competitiveness and cementing art and design with national, strategic importance in the US. On this occasion Professor Kataoka responded to Dr Maeda's accomplishments saying, "I got a lot done in my third quarter, John. So don't waste yours."[7]

A new style of leadership

As a newly installed president, Dr Maeda was aware of books written about the first 90 days of a new job, which tended to recommend the same thing: as a new leader you should not have a vision until you have listened to the relevant stakeholders. However, Dr Maeda recalls the first question the media and people associated with RISD wanted to ask was "what is your vision?"

Recurring questions included "Are you bringing technology to RISD?" To which Dr Maeda responded, "No, I'm bringing RISD to technology." Laying out a broad-based vision for RISD during his inaugural address, Dr Maeda said the school should "rise to the challenge" of the digital era "because we can."[8]

Another of Dr Maeda's early goals was to establish a more open form of leadership, which engendered him to supporters—mainly the student population and their parents—but also drew detractors, mostly from RISD's faculty.

As an example, in the first month of his presidency, when the new intake of freshmen arrived with their parents for what is commonly known as "move in day," wearing a T-shirt and shorts, Dr Maeda joined other volunteers to unload boxes from the long line of vehicles and help students move into their dormitories. Dr Maeda explains that he saw the day as an opportunity to talk to parents and students and learn about their motivations and expectations for studying at RISD. For example, this is how he learned that many parents were not sending their sons and daughters to RISD to become artists, but to become innovators and entrepreneurs. From talking to parents and students, Dr Maeda also detected that RISD provided a sense of belonging; a place where students, many of whom had struggled to find their place in the world, could fit in. Crucially, RISD was a place where students and their parents felt that achieving anything was possible.

This concept was further endorsed during a presentation Dr Maeda made to students and their parents to gauge their response to some of his new ideas for RISD to focus on. The plan was for the audience to applaud the ideas they liked. Following a tepid response to the first few proposals, when Dr Maeda said a goal was "building a justifiable case for creativity in the world," he immediately received an enthusiastic response.

"It scored off the charts," Dr Maeda recalls.

Soon after the meeting had ended, he was approached by a student who told him, as an art student who felt that no one took her seriously, just how much that vision meant to her. "I'm moved," she said, "because you said you would fight for us."

For Dr Maeda this was also an uplifting moment. "It was special. What she said drove me forward," he says.[9]

The RISD Board of Trustees, who hired Dr Maeda, were also upbeat about his initial performance. "I think he's a phenomenal choice," RISD trustee and Bank Rhode Island CEO Merrill Sherman was quoted as saying in *The Providence Journal* in June 2008 under the headline "RISD's Rock Star."

"In terms of vision, breadth of experience and the ability to communicate with different kinds of people, he was head and shoulders above anyone else who applied for the job," Sherman added. "Like it or not, the future is going to be dominated by technology. With John, we get the best of both worlds—an artist who's also at home with technology."[10]

Dr Maeda demonstrated his intentions to establish a more open form of leadership in other ways. He introduced "Jogging with John," a semi-weekly run in which faculty and students joined him for an after-dark run around the campus. Meanwhile, often to the complete astonishment of parents and their sons and daughters alike, he called the top 100 students who had been accepted to study at RISD each year. However, what was intended to be a congratulatory call turned out to be a surprising revelation. While the students he called had achieved the required grades to study at RISD, more than 90% would not be able to do so because they lacked the necessary finances. This was further highlighted by a potential student who told Dr Maeda that she had wanted to study at RISD since she was 12 years old, and what it meant to her to be accepted, but for financial reasons would attend another college that had offered her a full scholarship.

These conversations with students who were unable to study at RISD due to financial constraints became a catalyst for Dr Maeda to focus on expanding the scope of scholarships, which included setting up his own Maeda Family six-figure scholarship, as he was determined to change the way financial aid was offered.[11]

Dr Maeda explains that establishing the Maeda Family scholarship made it easier to ask potential donors to contribute to scholarship funding. As a co-investor, Dr Maeda says he was in a position to ask, "Why don't you give together with me?" Importantly, because of what RISD was able to offer, Dr Maeda felt emboldened to seek scholarship funding. "It's harder to raise funds for something that isn't really good. And I thought I had a really good product to raise funds for," he says.[12]

Cementing relationships

Believing you never truly understand your business and how it can be improved until you form strong connections with customers and the people you work with, as president Dr Maeda promised students that they would see him often. True to his word, he frequently walked around the campus talking to students and asking for their comments on various aspects of the school. He even made a point of eating in the RISD student cafeterias and dining halls.

Dr Maeda termed this as "conducting customer research." Unlike many colleges that viewed the faculty as the customer and the Board of Trustees as the investor, in Dr Maeda's view the opposite applied: students were the customer and parents were the investors.

Dr Maeda also liked to spend time or "hang out" with the RISD groundskeepers and food services staff. He would even take a turn serving food to staff and students including delivering donuts to campus security staff.

"I did this because I felt it was important to learn everything I could about how the university worked and why everyone is important and everyone's contribution can make a difference."

To help foster communication and collaborative interconnection, one of Dr Maeda's first university-wide initiatives was to replace the RISD legacy email system, which frequently crashed, with Google Apps. Recalling his early days as president, Dr Maeda remembers that students complained how they were tired of receiving emails from the administration that spoke about the importance of community and communication, but the end of each email would read, "Please do not reply to this message."

Confident he could improve the situation, Dr Maeda began leveraging the communication methods he knew well—such as email and blogging. He also found that using social media platforms gave him the opportunity to have an online forum where he could share different thoughts and ideas he was forming. To record how students felt when they learned they had been accepted to study at RISD, Dr Maeda kept a collage of Twitter printouts on a wall in his office. One outpouring of joy he pinned on his wall read "My friend got into RISD, bless her butt." Another simply read "Shhhhhhhhhhhzzzzzzzzzzzz aaaaaaaaaaaaaaaammmmmmmmmm!"

In a blog Dr Maeda began a year after taking up the presidency at RISD, which he described as a place where he could "think out loud," he wrote, "Leading people is quite different. Everything takes at least twice as long as you expect, if you are lucky. Iteration equals disruption."[13] At the time, Dr Maeda was one of a few college presidents to have a personal Facebook page. Furthermore, he was a habitual tweeter, using the then-limit of 140 characters to share insights and dictums on leadership and creativity.

Dr Maeda's fondness for using X (formerly known as Twitter) became a talking point among other university leaders. Relatively early in his presidency, Dr Maeda remembers attending an event for university presidents where a fellow president informed Dr Maeda that his presence on social media platforms was attracting considerable interest from college academics. Dr Maeda was slightly bemused when the president said, "Actually, we are waiting for you to fail," in a "we know how this will end" tone of voice.

Undeterred by the attention of his peers, in addition to his president's blog, which he used to encourage people to communicate with the president's office, Dr Maeda instituted Anonymous Tuesdays, where members of the RISD community could convey their views and opinions, providing they refrained from making personal attacks. While Dr Maeda's communication and presidential style was welcomed by many, it also attracted pushback, including from those who felt his bold choice of hands-on leadership was unorthodox to the point it undermined the status attached to being the president of RISD.

"I thought about this every year I helped students move into their dorms on 'move in day,' but I always felt the positives outweighed any perceived negatives," Dr Maeda notes about his approach to leadership.[14]

Unorthodox choices

In a similar way that Dr Maeda was prepared to make bold choices, RISD was founded on intrepid and somewhat unorthodox choices. What would arguably become the nation's top arts and design school was established and nurtured by a small group of women long before women in the US had the right to vote.

In 1876, Helen Adelia Rowe Metcalf urged 34 members of the Rhode Island Women's Centennial Commission to invest their group's surplus funding of $1,675—which they had raised for Rhode Island's contribution to the Philadelphia Centennial Exhibition—to found a school of art and design, instead of building a public fountain, which was one of the other proposed options. The objective behind establishing RISD was driven by the desire to support Rhode Island's thriving textiles and jewelry industries. To help meet in demand skills, the first courses offered at RISD were focused on two main areas: freehand drawing and painting and mechanical drawing and design.[15]

Demanding times demand a new approach

Similar to the sentiment of "yes we can" that marked a sense of hope for many at the beginning of President Barack Obama's time in office, the optimism that Dr Maeda brought to RISD was about to be challenged. Dr Maeda's early days at RISD coincided with the 2008–2009 global financial crises, which resulted in the most layoffs in RISD's 130-year history. Without pushing the presidential connection with President Barack Obama too far, Dr Maeda says, the global financial crises meant it was a tough time to be a president of anything.

Facing major economic challenges, including the income from endowments drying up, Dr Maeda was forced to find a way to balance a budget that would ensure salaries were paid, buildings maintained, and student education was impacted as little as possible. Like most things in life that involve making difficult decisions that have widespread implications, Dr Maeda says the experience of running a university is something that needs to be lived firsthand.

"I had to learn to be RISD's president in some of the hardest financial times for the school. It taught me lessons about the hard realities of running a university and how to figure things out."

Dr Maeda says the experience was demanding and challenging, but in a strangely wonderful way. "It broke me, it destroyed me, but I became a better person and president because of it."

The experience reminded him of a presidential training camp he attended at Harvard before he took up the position at RISD. In particular, he remembers a presentation on leadership by a respected expert in the field who told the 60 or so new presidents of universities, colleges, and community colleges from around the world that everything they needed to know about leadership was in the video he was about to present. Expecting a slick presentation with standout graphics and "10 points of leadership" crafted in easy-to-remember bullets, when the lights dimmed Dr Maeda was surprised to see black and white images of Dr Martin Luther King, Jr delivering his renowned "I Have a Dream" speech. As the lights in the room came back on, Dr Maeda recalls that the presidents sat in a stunned silence because they realized that leadership is not about the leader, but about the scale of the challenges that the leader will face. Dr Maeda would soon find this to be true when the changes he proposed to the long-established structure of the traditional RISD curriculum made him deeply unpopular with the RISD faculty.[16]

Favorite failure

Having weathered the fallout of the global financial crisis and guided RISD back to a firm operating footing, a foreshadowing prophecy that Dr Maeda often refers to manifested: "When things seem as good as they are going to get, for sure they will start to go wrong." Similar to his predecessor Roger Mandle, who stepped down after receiving a vote of no confidence from RISD department heads in 2007, in 2011 Dr Maeda received pushback from faculty members after he proposed making changes to the RISD curriculum. Under a plan entitled "Connecting the Dots," Dr Maeda and his team suggested changes that included decreasing the number of credits required to graduate—from 126 to 120—as well as giving emphasis to interdisciplinary courses that aimed to integrate art into developing economic fields. The belief being that such changes would make RISD graduates more employable upon graduation.

"The proposals made me very unpopular among the faculty," says Dr Maeda. He also received criticism for his tech-centric leadership style that faculty members said substituted genuine dialog for social media conceits.[17]

Inside Higher Ed reported that RISD faculty members argued that the administration's new strategic plan placed so much emphasis on interdisciplinary work that key disciplines—especially in the fine arts—were losing their essential role.[18] On February 23, 2011, the faculty rejected the draft plan.

"The entire faculty voted no confidence in me," Dr Maeda recalls.

In an email to RISD constituents addressing the concerns raised by the faculty, Dr Maeda said he took the no confidence vote as a clear sign that he had to redouble his efforts to build a strong relationship with faculty members. In a move to improve relations between the faculty and administration, the plan to merge the Division of Fine Arts and the Division of Architecture and Design was withdrawn. However, the RISD Board of Trustees "unanimously endorsed in concept the draft and continuation of the planning process" for the "Connecting the Dots" proposal.

"Collectively, the initiatives in this draft plan ensure that RISD will continue to be a preeminent institution of art and design education, solidly positioning us for the future by strengthening our academic core and enriching opportunities for our students," Dr Maeda wrote in a statement released to the RISD community.[19]

In response to the vote of no confidence, Dr Maeda initiated open office hours for faculty, staff, and students. He said at the time, though they were not always easy conversations, they made him feel grateful to be part of a community that felt so passionately about its future.[20] With full support from the RISD Board of Trustees and the majority of students, with various concessions made and communication with faculty improved, Dr Maeda survived the vote of no confidence.

"I was one of one percent of college presidents in the year of 2011 who received a no confidence vote that managed to survive," Dr Maeda recalls. Shortly after surviving the vote of no confidence, he was contacted by the leadership training department of the US Central Intelligence Agency (CIA) who asked about the strategies he used to survive the vote of no confidence.

With hindsight, reflecting on what led to the vote of no confidence situation, Dr Maeda realizes he focused too much on the students and not enough on the faculty.

"I'm okay with that. I turned it around, righted the institution, and was able to put the business model back together to bring RISD back to number one," says Dr Maeda.

Commenting on the lessons he learned from the experience, he says being the president of RISD is not about the individual; it is about the students, faculty, and the community. "It was tough, but it was a good experience. In some ways it was my favorite failure. And so I began to learn how to be on behalf of the community. I became someone else."

Dr Maeda adds that artists and designers are adept at figuring things out. "You stumble, pick yourself up, and keep going," he says.

Another important lesson Dr Maeda learned was how people generally are comfortable with the way things are, and they do not want the work that change brings, even if change means tangible benefits. It reminded Dr Maeda of a quote by General Eric Shinseki, the first Asian American four-star general and the first Asian American Secretary of Veterans Affairs, who said, "If you don't like change, you're going to like irrelevance even less."[21]

Meanwhile, three years into his tenure as RISD president, he had reason to be thankful his family had remained in Massachusetts, when grievances aired by RISD's faculty against Dr Maeda's administration became a divisive publicly discussed topic.

"I was relieved my children were distanced from the conversations taking place in the small college town," Dr Maeda says.

Even though his children lived in another state, they were not entirely immune to the resentment some people felt towards their father. While his eldest daughter was attending a summer camp activity, a teacher who realized who her father was called her away from her friends and told her that her father was "a very bad man."

At the time Dr Maeda was navigating the repercussions of the vote of no confidence, positive things were gaining widespread attention including the recognition RISD was receiving as the leading advocate for the STEM-to-STEAM movement.

"My doubters were kind of like, how can John be a failure and a success at the same time?" Dr Maeda recalls.[22]

From STEM to STEAM

Among Dr Maeda's noteworthy accomplishments at RISD, one that gained particular widespread recognition is the movement he spearheaded to transform the focus on STEM (science, technology, engineering, and math) education to STEAM, by adding art. Underpinned by his belief that "art and design are poised to transform world economies in the 21st century just as science and technology did in the 20th century"[23]— an observation Dr Maeda first made during his interview to become president of RISD—under Dr Maeda's leadership, RISD became a focal point in the campaign to propagate the STEM-to-STEAM movement nationally.

"It was probably the most significant thing I moved into action at RISD," says Dr Maeda.

In a similar way that MIT was a leader in advancements in science and technology after World War II that contributed to improvements in the American quality of life and strengthening the US economy, Dr Maeda believed through art and design RISD could alter the course of the country for good.

"I felt a kind of audacity that RISD could achieve this for the country," Dr Maeda says.

With this in mind, in 2010, RISD began to champion the addition of art and design to the national agenda of education and research to develop a comprehensive educational model that would better prepare future generations to compete in the 21st century innovation economy.

While he was not the first person to advocate for STEAM, because he straddled the worlds of technology, art, and design, and as the president of RISD, Dr Maeda believes he was in a unique position to articulate the benefits of STEAM from a cross-disciplinary perspective. However, it was not a case of simply adding art to STEM, but more of incorporating art to illuminate the "who and why," the reasoning, to the "what and how" of STEM. Put simply, STEAM incorporates the benefits of STEM in and through the arts in an authentic way for a more complete, well-rounded education.

"After many years crisscrossing the fields of technology, art, and design, I came to the conclusion while there is great power in STEM and art when taken separately, but have even more power when both fields come together," says Dr Maeda.

He also championed the growing connection between art, design, and entrepreneurship, coining the word "artrepreneurship" to denote the type of businesses artists and designers tend to found. Importantly, the STEM-to-STEAM initiative received the support of the parents of RISD students who saw the alignment between STEAM education and job creation.

"Even wealthy parents who can afford to support their children like to see them get good jobs," notes Dr Maeda. "It seemed like turning STEM to STEAM made a lot of sense."

For instance, he began to think about art and the relationship of art to different fields, ranging from design and industry to economics.

One of Dr Maeda's additional motivating factors for advancing the STEM-to-STEAM movement was his observation that across the United States, art classes, particularly in the junior and high school education landscape, were disappearing, in part to fund STEM programs or STEM-related facilities such as chemistry labs. At a time when Dr Maeda considered the cross-pollination of art, science, and technology could not be more crucial, parents were reporting the time their children were receiving art education was being reduced.

"I thought that STEAM could help to address the misalignment of resources nationally," Dr Maeda notes.[24]

Nevertheless, among art educators there was a divide between those who embraced the STEM-to-STEAM model and those that rebutted it because they did not see the necessity for art to be recognized as an intersection with science and technology.

As the "face," or as he was sometimes described, the "driving policy entrepreneur" behind the STEM-to-STEAM movement, Dr Maeda forged relationships within local, national, and international arenas.

With his colleague Babette Allina, who was then the Director of Government Relations at RISD, Dr Maeda, with a "little persuasion" as he describes it, managed to gain support for the STEM-to-STEAM movement from Rhode Island Congressman Jim Langevin, who subsequently introduced the potential impact on US education and innovation to fellow members of Congress.[25] At a briefing sponsored by RISD held on Capitol Hill in February 2013, Congresswoman Suzanne Bonamici (D-OR) and Congressman Aaron Schock (R-IL) announced the formation of the Congressional STEAM (STEM+Arts and Design) Caucus. The group said it would host briefings and advocate for policy changes that would encourage educators to integrate arts, broadly defined, with traditional science, technology, engineering, and math curriculum.[26]

From the East Coast to the West Coast and across the United States, elected officials of differing political persuasions greeted the STEM-to-STEAM concept with enthusiasm. As a culmination of political effort, the STEM-to-STEAM movement achieved a landmark moment with the inclusion of STEAM in the federal Every Student Succeeds Act (ESSA)—which superseded No Child Left Behind (P.L.114-95, 2015). Another important piece of legislation, the America Competes Reauthorization Act

Dr Maeda advocating for the STEM-to-STEAM movement on Capitol Hill

of 2015, integrated STEAM into federal STEM programming, research, and innovation activities.

Offering an insight as to why the STEAM concept received favorable bipartisan acceptance, Dr Maeda explains, "It was a timely topic that wasn't controversial and offered a broad appeal."

Dr Maeda on stage at the John F. Kennedy Center for the Performing Arts with Bob Lynch, former president and CEO of Americans for the Arts, and Rep. Suzanne Bonamici, co-chair of the Congressional STEAM Caucus

Even the Sesame Workshop, best known for producing the iconic children's educational television program *Sesame Street*, in 2012 updated its longstanding STEM curriculum to STEAM as a means of reinforcing the ongoing value of the arts and humanities.[27]

For his work in championing STEAM education, in 2013 Dr Maeda was recognized with a Tribeca Disruptive Innovation Award. Dr Maeda received further recognition in 2016 when he was invited to deliver the keynote presentation at the Nancy

Hanks Lecture on Arts & Public Policy at the Kennedy Center, Washington, D.C. Dr Maeda recalls, wherever they took place, STEM-to-STEAM events attracted such a large audience that often there was standing room only.[28]

Connecting STEM and STEAM to real-world issues

Throughout history, while art and science have often been tied together, as someone who has a foot in both camps, Dr Maeda is aware of the challenges that bringing art and science together can create. To a large extent, he says, while the two disciplines involve inquisitiveness, they both require a different mindset. For example, a scientific mind needs to turn off distractions to focus, while the artistic mindset needs to embrace divergence to open up to new things.

"Both artists and scientists are introverts, but artists and designers like to introvert together," quips Dr Maeda.

For the rare group of people who try to intersect between the arts and science, the pressure to commit to one or the other can be intense.

"It can be very hard to switch context," says Dr Maeda.

He recalls his own youth, when his teachers praised him for being good at math and art. His father, however, would tell friends and family of Dr Maeda's aptitude for mathematics, but often left out his penchant for the arts. "I always wondered why art and science were considered different, making me feel I had to choose between the two," he says.

As an advocate for the collaborative potential that exists when artists and designers combine forces with engineers, during STEM-to-STEAM keynote presentations and interviews Dr Maeda frequently pointed out that artists and designers are the ones who help bring humanity to the forefront by seeking answers that resonate with human values. At the time when he was championing the STEM-to-STEAM movement, to make his case, Dr Maeda would often cite the MP3 player as a classic example of a technology that while functional, lacked desirability, until Apple "humanized" it in the iPod by combining elegance with function. Dr Maeda also cites the world-renowned entertainment show, Cirque du Soleil, which incorporates multimedia productions and immersive experiences, as a prime example of STEAM concepts coming together, which is particularly pertinent as the company's chief technology officer in 2003 was a RISD graduate. "Cirque du Soleil is total STEAM," says Dr Maeda.[29]

Dr Maeda argues while STEM by itself is extremely powerful, alone it lacks the ingredient to create warmth and connection with humanity. The arts, Dr Maeda explains, teach society to empathize, to create, to collaborate, and to humanize. He also makes the case that critical thinking, critical making, and creative leadership lead to an enlightened form of innovation— one where art, design, technology, and the world of business intersect. Explaining what he perceives as the difference between STEM and STEAM, Dr Maeda says scientific thinking or the scientific method is critical of the experiment, but not its impact on humanity, whereas the arts tend to focus on the human spirit, human culture, moral elements, and effects on society.

Dr Maeda believes he was fortunate to have grown up in an era of scientists who realized the importance of art and the humanities. Referring to Professor Jerome Wiesner, who was a co-founder of the Media Lab and served as president of MIT from 1971 to 1980, Dr Maeda says Professor Wiesner was an example of a post-World War II era scientist who later turned his attention to the humanities. Involved with the top-secret Manhattan Project to make the first atomic bombs during World War II, after the war, as chairman of the Science Advisory Committee, which provided advice to President John F. Kennedy, Professor Wiesner was a strong advocate for a nuclear test ban treaty on the grounds that nuclear weapons tests were a clear threat to the environment and to human health. As president of MIT, Professor Wiesner oversaw a policy that required for every MIT campus construction project, the equivalent of 1% of the budget should be invested in the arts. Dr Maeda says it was Professor Wiesner's belief that "scientists and engineers must be steeped in humanistic learning" that shaped his philosophy that "humanist technologists" could make a profound difference as engineer-designers and engineer-artists.[30]

History and art are interwoven with STEAM

From cave drawings of animals that help today's researchers to understand ancient ecosystems, to centuries-old paintings depicting scientific experiments, visual art has been used for thousands of years to express scientific knowledge. While his *Mona Lisa* is probably the most famous portrait ever painted, Leonardo da Vinci's work as an artist, engineer, inventor, and student of all things scientific is one of the most well-known examples of the intersection between art and science. In more recent times, before photography became a popular way of illustrating the natural world, Dr Maeda points out that people such as the naturalist, geologist, and biologist Charles Darwin—best known for developing the theory of evolution by natural selection—were both scientists and artists.

"Charles Darwin's sketches of plants are both detailed and beautiful," notes Dr Maeda.

Making the point that exploring nature is intrinsically interdisciplinary, Dr Maeda highlights that, for many years RISD's Edna W. Lawrence Nature Lab with its vast collection of taxidermy animals, plants, and mineral materials has embodied the STEAM concept by bringing together artists, designers, and scientists with the goal of fostering multiple modes of inquiry.[31] Founded by RISD faculty member Edna Lawrence in the early 20th century to "open students' eyes to the marvels of beauty in nature … of forms, space, color, texture, design and structure,"[32] in an effort to build online STEAM teaching resources from pre-K to grade 12, the Nature Lab and the RISD Museum partnered with PBS Learning Media, a free, web-based collection of multimodal learning resources, searchable by subject area.

At the same time, STEAM advocacy efforts brought in funding to RISD from new partners including the National Science Foundation and the Robert Wood Johnson Foundation, which funded the *Make It Better* initiative, which supports artists and designers to engage with issues of health and wellness in innovative and unexpected ways. In 2012, RISD launched the inaugural class of Maharam STEAM Fellows in Applied Art and Design, which funds RISD students to pursue internships in the public and nonprofit sectors. Dr Maeda also set aside space close to the president's office to accommodate a student-led STEAM think tank headed by Babette Allina, the Director of Government Relations at RISD. RISD was among the first schools to partner with a number of unique organizations: Upstart, an AI platform that works with banks and credit unions to use non-traditional variables, such as education and employment to predict creditworthiness; Quirky, a now-defunct invention platform that connected inventors with companies;[33] global online marketplace Etsy; and Square, which makes a point-of-sale system and services for payment processing software and hardware.

A lasting legacy

Today, STEAM practices are embedded across RISD's curriculum from the Brown–RISD Dual Degree program and research in the Co-Works Research Lab and the Nature Lab to graduate degree programs such as Digital+Media and a longstanding cross-discipline partnership with the NASA Studio in Industrial Design. Although no longer in operation, RISD also set up a mapping tool (map.stemtosteam.org) that visualized STEAM activity worldwide to enable advocates, practitioners, and followers of the movement to connect with each other, share best practices, and show decision makers the impact and relevance of art and design.

In the years since Dr Maeda began the campaign to propagate the STEM-to-STEAM movement, the concept has been widely adopted by institutions, corporations, and leaders globally.

"I'm pleased that the experiment worked and resulted in a win."

However, Dr Maeda acknowledges his personal connection to the STEAM movement has largely been forgotten. Not that an absence of recognition for his achievements particularly bothers him. Instead, he prefers to quote the wisdom of Lao Tzu—thought to have been an older contemporary of Confucius—who proposed that a leader is best when people barely know he exists; when his work is done, his aim fulfilled, they will say: we did it ourselves.[34]

Memorable meeting

As the president of RISD, Dr Maeda met many people who introduced him to new ways of thinking and topics he was inspired to explore. Dr Maeda recalls one such memorable meeting with world-famous cellist and virtuoso Yo-Yo Ma, when they had a conversation about the "edge effect," the point where two ecosystems or cultures meet and new life systems emerge and creativity is generated. For example, where the forest and the savannah intersect or artists and musicians from different cultures and different traditions come together, resulting in new areas of creativity.

Having cancelled a performance at RISD by Ma due to global financial crisis-related financial constraints, Dr Maeda was slightly apprehensive about meeting Ma in person. He had no need to be. Ma seemed either to have forgotten the cancellation or was too polite to mention it.

"Our conversation really stuck with me," Dr Maeda says.

As someone who traverses the boundaries between art and science, and at different times has been expected to choose between art and math, the concept of the "edge effect" continues to resonate strongly. Rejecting the idea that gulfs should exist between seemingly disparate fields or talent should be confined to one box, Dr Maeda empathizes with people who feel an affinity for the interplay between art and science, but are under pressure to align with one discipline or the other to avoid feeling they are doing something wrong.

"People know that they shouldn't have to choose, but find it is easier to choose to be a math person or an arts person than to live not knowing who they are," Dr Maeda says.

Applied in full to a university setting, the fuzzy lines of the "edge effect" would allow courses to overlap and meander through the curriculum. However, he feels it will be some time, if ever, before this happens.

"There is a tendency in academia to allow two courses to overlap, but not allow other courses to kiss," Dr Maeda notes. With this in mind, similar to the "edge effect," Dr Maeda is encouraged by the way that many young people embrace blending or "intersectionality," which is usually associated with race and gender identity. "Young people are teaching us what 'blending' means; unfortunately, the world they are entering is not."[35]

A fresh look at leadership

Ironically, at the same time that his leadership decisions were being called in to question by the RISD faculty, writing as an artist and designer, a technologist, and a professor, Dr Maeda's fifth book, *Redesigning Leadership*, was published by MIT Press in April 2011.

Explaining that he wrote *Redesigning Leadership* to better understand the role of leadership, Dr Maeda says he was looking for ways to come to terms with not having all the answers or the immediate solutions to the leadership challenges he faced.

"Leadership hurts," Dr Maeda says. "The responsibility of leadership can feel like a stiletto heel pressing on your chest with the pressure of an elephant. You can't get rid of it; sometimes you feel that you can't breathe."

Dr Maeda explains that *Redesigning Leadership* is not about how to lead, but more of a summation of ideas and challenges based on his own experiences of leadership failures and success as he tried to balance his creative artistic instincts with his formal training in engineering and business management. The challenge, he says, was trying to understand how to remain creative as a leader of a system and, at the same time, how to avoid becoming just another leader.

"There was a lot of experimentation," he says.

His leadership learning journey included well-intentioned decisions that sometimes resulted in unexpected consequences. As such, the vignettes featured in *Redesigning Leadership* focus on trial and error and retrial that reflect the way leadership is practiced and experienced in the real world. For example, Dr Maeda explains why he believes it is a sign of strength instead of a weakness when leaders to show their human side as well as their business-driven objectives while adhering to their principles.

"If you compromise your integrity and principles on minor issues, it gets easier to make bad choices on the big issues."

The book also explores how leaders need to be able to accept constructive criticism and reflect on it in order to improve. Dr Maeda recommends that leaders should have the courage to acknowledge what they do not know, observing that "competency that results in success can lead to complacency, which can result in failure, which can progress to learning how to be competent again." Offering another piece of advice, Dr Maeda recommends whenever possible, leaders should get to know their people as human beings first and colleagues or employees second. For instance, Dr Maeda suggests that, when an individual becomes a leader they should not forget they are still a human being, too. He recommends that leaders should live by their ideals, connect with their employees in personal ways, and communicate as clearly as possible.

Writing *Redesigning Leadership* also led to Dr Maeda becoming curious about the less explored characteristics of leadership. For example, like an artist or a sculptor, a leader can feel isolated and lonely. He also observed that creative people who make things ("makers") tend to make poor leaders. The premise being because "makers" tend to solve problems for themselves, they are less likely to rely on others to provide solutions. On the other hand, non-makers who are not natural problem solvers need to work with other people to solve problems. This requires a different set of competencies that gravitate towards charisma, strong communication skills, and an engaging personality.

On the topic of whether leaders are born or nurtured, Dr Maeda believes it is a combination of both, however, with a few requisites. While leaders usually owe their leadership strengths to their cognitive abilities, experience, personality, and communication skills, taller people, according to Dr Maeda, have an advantage if they choose to become a leader.[36]

Citing research conducted by Nancy Blaker and several colleagues,[37] this idea is based on the evolutionary perspective that taller individuals are seen as more leader-like because they are perceived as more dominant, healthy, and intelligent. In ancestral human environments being fit and physically imposing were arguably important leadership qualities— possibly more so for males—where being a leader entailed considerable physical risks. Expanding on the evolutionary theory, Dr Maeda believes, although he admits it might not be scientifically proven, if a person is tall, male, white, and comes from a well-off background with access to higher education and a network of influential connections, they have an advantage if they choose to become a leader.

In addition to learning on-the-job leadership skills, Dr Maeda notes how he benefited from the insights of others. He recalls attending a leadership forum where Professor Marshall Ganz, Senior Lecturer in Leadership, Organizing, and Civil Society at Harvard Kennedy School was speaking, although initially he admits to not expecting too much. However, having recently bought a new iPhone, Dr Maeda instinctively hit "record" when the lecture began.

"While president of RISD I listened to Marshall Ganz's one-hour presentation every day while I made and ate my breakfast—and the many lessons in it sunk in, and gave sense to me why my storytelling over the years 'worked' and why it sometimes didn't work, too," Dr Maeda recalls.

Explaining how authority and leadership are not the same thing, Professor Ganz said leadership is about enabling others to achieve shared purpose under conditions of uncertainty.

"What he said has stayed with me," Dr Maeda says.

Professor Ganz also explained how leaders who are driving change often have the skills to weave a compelling story that combines self, us, and now. The story of "self" is about the individual and the individual's journey to become who you are today. Ideally it is a story that others can relate to in some way, even if the details are slightly different. Meanwhile, the story of "us" is about the people who are listening to the story and why they are connected and integral to the topic or outcome. The story of "now" is a chance to seize the moment of opportunity to highlight how the leader is facilitating and guiding people to better outcomes and how they would not be able get there without the leader.[38]

New horizons

With lessons learned from the vote of no confidence, under Dr Maeda's leadership the following year in 2012 RISD was ranked number one in *Business Insider's* survey of The World's 25 Best

Design Schools.[39] At the same time applications increased by 9.4% in 2012 and increased a further 3.5% in 2013. As a result, RISD was able to enroll the most diverse undergraduate classes in its history, thanks in part to increases in financial aid which in 2014 meant that three-quarters of accepted freshmen with a proven need were offered financial aid compared with just one-third two years previously. In addition, enabled by donations, long-deferred renovations commenced on the historic Illustration Studies Building, which houses RISD's largest and most interdisciplinary department.[40]

After six years as president at RISD, during which time he had elevated the role art and design play in engineering, technology, and manufacturing, Dr Maeda felt the need to explore new opportunities. Likening himself to a green tomato on the path to ripening, Dr Maeda said he was wary of becoming a fully ripened red tomato, which only has one way to go: decay and fade away.

He was also motivated by RISD alumnus Joe Gebbia, co-founder of Airbnb, who during presentations to students at the college would talk about taking the next step.

"I would invite Joe Gebbia to talk to the students because he was so inspiring. He was an important person to hear because he was one of them; he was a designer."

Dr Maeda explains how Gebbia would always begin his presentations by saying four words, "Take the next step."

"I realized he was not only talking to the students, he was talking to me," Dr Maeda reveals. "I heard what he was saying."

Having developed and maintained close ties with Silicon Valley, Dr Maeda was fascinated by how start-up companies are formed and how they grow.

"I knew I couldn't fully learn how start-ups grew and functioned by remaining a college president," he says.

However, it took one of his most vocal critics on campus to finally push him into making the decision to leave. As Dr Maeda recalls, the naysayer approached him and said: "John, I know we gave you a hard time, but everything is fine now, so you finally get to take it easy."

"Take it easy? Quite frankly the thought lacked appeal," Dr Maeda says. "Again I heard the four words: 'Take the next step'." With his decision to leave RISD made, Dr Maeda activated a succession plan to hand over the presidency to Rosanne Somerson, a successful woodworker, furniture designer/maker, and educator he had recruited into the RISD leadership ranks.[41]

In the farewell message he made for the RISD campus community, Dr Maeda noted that he was "so proud to have been part of this community—to have led it, to have built an amazing academic and operational team, and to have represented it in the world. I know that I leave RISD as the best art and design school in the world and with the opportunity that it will be even better in the years to come."[42]

04

A Fresh Start in
Silicon Valley

Responsibilities and challenges

In 2013, when Dr Maeda made the transition from academia to the high-tech world of Silicon Valley, his objective was to continue his passion for work at the intersection of design, technology, and business. As the first design partner with Kleiner Perkins Caufield & Byers (KPCB; now known as Kleiner Perkins), the venture capital (VC) firm that helped to launch Amazon and Google, Dr Maeda's role focused on working with KPCB's entrepreneurs and portfolio companies to "build design DNA into their company cultures," according to the firm.[1]

Sometimes Dr Maeda worked with KPCB's investment partners and other times with the CEO of a portfolio company to give a tutorial on how design and engineering can be combined to achieve strategic outcomes. Dr Maeda was also tasked to lead KPCB's Design Council, a group of a dozen or so Silicon Valley designers that brought together mentors and upcoming design talent in the technology industry. In addition, Dr Maeda worked with KPCB's Design Fellows mentorship program which was launched in 2012 to support internships for college students at start-up firms. Similar to MIT where Dr Maeda had championed technologists who aspired to be artists and designers, and at RISD where he had championed artists and designers who sought to be technologists, in his new role in the VC community, he focused on supporting and raising the profile of designers who were transforming the technology and start-up ecosystem.

The realization he was walking through the same KPCB office doors as well-known entrepreneurs was not lost on Dr Maeda. Larry Page and Sergey Brin, best known for co-founding Google, and Jeff Bezos, founder, executive chairman, and former president and CEO of Amazon, had all sought financing from KPCB. The connection resonated with Dr Maeda's interest in how money could be used as a medium; especially how money could lead to the formation of a new business from a spark of imagination by people who believe the impossible could be made possible.

As if he had not taken on enough new responsibilities, Dr Maeda also became chair of the eBay Design Advisory Board, working with the company to evolve its design capabilities by elevating the relevance of designers. In working with a mature company like eBay, Dr Maeda says his intention was to better understand the end-to-end evolution of a tech company, and at the same time work with companies during their start-up stage, with the possibility that one day these companies could become the next eBay.

However, if Dr Maeda was expecting a seamless pivot from leading a prominent university to joining the future-

Dr Maeda at the American Institute of Graphic Arts San Francisco in his role as chair of eBay's Design Advisory Board. Also pictured are Uris Dacosta (left), then Vice President of Design at PayPal; John Donahoe (second from left), then eBay CEO; and Dane Howard (right), then eBay's Director of Global Brand Experience & Design.

focused world of Silicon Valley, he was about to encounter an abrupt awakening.

"Boy, was I unprepared," he explains.

While he found his tenure at RISD emotionally challenging, for Dr Maeda the move to Silicon Valley was intellectually demanding. In the six years since leaving the cutting edge of technology at MIT to become president of RISD, the world of technology in general, and in Silicon Valley in particular, had taken an exponential leap.

"I felt like the Rip van Winkle of technology," Dr Maeda recalls, referring to the fictional character created by American author Washington Irving who falls asleep after drinking strong alcohol and wakes up 20 years later to a much-changed world.

In hindsight, Dr Maeda says it took him the best part of five years to make up for the time he had spent away from the field of technology. "I was no longer clinging on to the side of the pool; I was swimming in the deep end."

Regardless of the fact that he had switched back and forth between the design and tech worlds for the best part of three decades—advising numerous companies in the process—Dr Maeda recalls feeling as if he had become the student and the people he was working with were the professors.

"I had a lot of catching up to do," he says.

He had moved from a place where he had faced tough, but manageable challenges, to an unfamiliar environment where he faced challenges which required "uphill thinking," a progression that Dr Maeda explains requires taking the "hard path" but relishing the challenge. For example, while many of his new experiences were inspiring, at the same time they could be intimidating. There were times, Dr Maeda recalls, when he saw what a young generation of designer/technologists were achieving and thought, "Wow, I'll never be like that." At other times inspiration would trigger his "audacity mode," which made him feel courageous and ready to confront challenges.

Even though the topic was never raised with him directly, through different sources, Dr Maeda became aware there was an element of scepticism concerning his ability to succeed in Silicon Valley. More specifically, there were those who doubted his ability to transition from the academic world to the high-tech commercial world. The fact that Dr Maeda had been both a student and a professor at MIT for close to 20 years and president of RISD for six years, which involved extensive collaboration with commercial partners, carried little weight with some people in Silicon Valley.

"Silicon Valley has always been more aligned with Stanford than MIT," Dr Maeda notes. While MIT is widely recognized as a hub for technological innovation, it is with Stanford University that Silicon Valley cemented a tradition of collaboration between academia and industry.

Dr Maeda says he was mainly comfortable with the scepticism because he understood why some might see him as an interloper.

"In most of the roles I took on, I was super naive at first," he says.

Until he established a measure of credibility, he had encountered a similar situation when he became president of RISD. During his early days at RISD, there were people that associated Dr Maeda with computer engineering instead of art and design.

Just as Dr Maeda showed his doubters at RISD he could succeed in the fields of art and design as well as technology and engineering, he felt motivated to prove his sceptics wrong. The situation reminded him of one of his favorite fortune cookie quotes, which reads: "The great pleasure of life is doing what other people say you cannot do." If not for the doubters, Dr Maeda says he probably would not have achieved some of the things he did.

"I did the hard work and it changed perceptions," he says. "It was what I needed to do to be accepted," he adds,[2] recalling Nelson Mandela's famous line "Do not judge me by my successes, judge me by how many times I fell down and got back up again."[3]

This involved transitioning from the leader of an intellectual institution to learning about the culture and leadership competencies required to put teams together to launch a start-up.

Another area Dr Maeda focused on was the challenges for design teams working in the high-tech industry. While the designer's role in a start-up is vital, Dr Maeda explains that the design component is one of a number of factors such as product sales and costs that need to be considered in the decision-making process. However, designers, Dr Maeda notes, tend to strive for absolute perfection, which can cause friction when the start-up world expects rapid and often imperfect iterations in order to scale-up prototypes and achieve swift commercialization. A catchphrase frequently heard at seminars, in board rooms, and in coffee shops in Silicon Valley where business meetings often took place was that "Ideas are cheap, execution is everything." As the KPCB design partner, as well as raising the profile of design, Dr Maeda sought to strengthen opportunities for designers to work with their colleagues as a team, which he believed would ultimately lead to better design.

In spite of the challenges Dr Maeda faced, there were some lighter moments. Early into his orientation period at KPCB, Dr Maeda remembers joining a meeting with his new colleagues. He thought they were watching CNN because on the screen, speaking live was Al Gore, the businessman and environmentalist who served as the 45th vice president of the United States. It took several minutes before Dr Maeda realized that Al Gore was actually participating in the KPCB meeting via webcam.[4]

Getting to grips with venture capital

Notwithstanding that Dr Maeda had completed his MBA, providing him with valuable insights into the various ways business finance works, it was only when he arrived in Silicon Valley that he realized how little he knew about how the VC industry operated.

"I had kind of heard about it, but I didn't really know what venture capital was all about," Dr Maeda says.

To improve his knowledge of VC funding, the solution, or so he thought, was to read a book titled *Creative Capital: Georges Doriot and the Birth of Venture Capital*. George Doriot, who founded the American Research and Development Corporation in 1946 and later became known as the "father of venture capitalism," is noted for the role he played in the formation of Digital Equipment Corporation, a major American company in the computer industry from the 1960s to the 1990s, and a number of other start-up companies that became success stories.[5] Although Dr Maeda enjoyed reading about George Doriot, it quickly became apparent that the VC landscape in the 1940s shared very few similarities to VC activities in 2013.

"It was a very different world," Dr Maeda says.

While he was aware of the different terminologies used to differentiate VC funding, he did not fully understand the complexities of the fundraising sequence. For example, how the seed and A, B, and C stages of fundraising each have a different level of risk and reward criteria. Dr Maeda was also unclear about the processes VC firms use to evaluate the funding mechanisms that make it possible for entrepreneurs, sometimes with limited or no experience of operating a business, to secure capital to launch a start-up.

To better understand the funding process, Dr Maeda thought of each stage as a growth hormone or the fuel that propels a rocket into space. The analogy being that like a rocket, start-ups can be difficult to launch and involve a high percentage of failures. This is when seed money faces the biggest risk. Once launched, indicating the rocket or start-up demonstrates a degree of reliability, the different levels of early funding are determined by the ratio of risk and reliability. When the rocket enters into space or when the start-up is beginning to establish a track record is when the late-stage funding is provided.

Dr Maeda also marveled at the amount and availability of funding for VC projects. For instance, he observed how it was commonplace for several start-ups with practically the same idea to raise funding from different sources at the same time. Firsthand insights also enabled Dr Maeda to set aside some misconceptions about the VC sector, such as that venture capitalists are only interested in making quick profits.

"People would say to me, venture capitalists are bad," he says, noting that good and bad people can be found in all walks of life. Considering that without VC funding the dream of launching a start-up might not become a reality, Dr Maeda says it was empowering to work in an environment that could make the seemingly impossible become possible.

"I think that's magic," he says, adding that people who have the funds to power start-ups are often the same people that want to make the world a better place.[6]

A change of circumstances

The transition from RISD to Silicon Valley also involved a significant change in Dr Maeda's lifestyle. In sharp contrast to the RISD President's House with its grand entryway and spacious rooms, Dr Maeda chose to spend the next three years living in Airbnb accommodation and using Uber for transport. An early user of Uber when it was first rolled out, Dr Maeda says by choosing Airbnbs he wanted to live like young people who were part of the gig and sharing economy. In one Airbnb where he stayed for an extended period of time, Dr Maeda was able to experience firsthand the drive and impulse involved in establishing a start-up company. He remembers how a noisy server was set up in the living room and the buzz of activity as young developers pooled their skills.

"The optimism was intoxicating," Dr Maeda recalls.

However, like many Silicon Valley start-ups, the start-up project Dr Maeda shared a domestic arrangement with failed. According to various venture capital and private equity databases that monitor VC activities, the failure rate for start-ups in Silicon Valley is about 90%, with as many as nine out of 10 start-ups failing within the first five years of being established.

Dr Maeda appreciates the outcome of another experience while staying in an Airbnb, although this one was unexpected and unwanted. Early one morning in 2015 while he was jogging near his home on El Camino Real, Dr Maeda tripped and fell, breaking his arm and badly bruising his face. Ironically,

Dr Maeda had recently published an article on *TechCrunch* about health tech. During the weeks following his accident, while he was somewhat incapacitated, Dr Maeda's Airbnb host family helped to nurse him back to health.

"I was very grateful," Dr Maeda says. "They were my second family on the West Coast."

Like when he was president at RISD, while he was based in Silicon Valley, Dr Maeda's wife and daughters remained in Lexington, Massachusetts, where his daughters were attending school. As well as living apart from his family, Dr Maeda also needed to adjust to no longer being the president of a prestigious university and the financial security the senior leadership position provided. In spite of any challenges he felt, Dr Maeda says there was no chance he would return to the world of academia. To go back, he explains, would have been self-defeating because it would have meant he was not taking the road forward to satisfy his curiosity.[7]

Diversity and inclusion

While academic thinking was less of a priority in Silicon Valley, an attribute that Dr Maeda was able to draw on from his many years as a professor and leader of a university was his strong sense of commitment to help others to thrive and succeed. A trait, Dr Maeda noted, that was not commonly found in the fast-paced world of business.

"I was seen as being a good manager of people, which I suppose you could say was something I was trained to do," Dr Maeda says. As a professor he had always made it his goal to help others achieve more than he had achieved himself, a philosophy that he continued to apply in his role as KPCB design partner.

As he became more familiar with the VC environment, Dr Maeda was also increasingly aware of a lack of inclusion and diversity. Instead of a cutting-edge technology environment populated by people of all genders from all walks of life, Dr Maeda noted an absence of different perspectives, particularly when it came to women and people of color.

"I felt I needed to make a conscious effort to change the situation by modifying my own activities," Dr Maeda explains. He did this by ensuring that more women and people of color were involved in the projects he was spearheading, which previously were often the domain of white males. During group meetings and interactions with different people, he pointed out how diverse perspectives can be invaluable when taking on a project or finding a solution to a challenge.

"I found that my conversations and gatherings became so much better when they were more diverse," Dr Maeda says. Notably, the feedback from participants in events and projects he led yielded some of the highest reviews within the company.[8] Dr Maeda adds that, when he was questioned about his diversity and inclusion efforts, he would jokingly say he wanted to avoid making an appearance on the "Congrats, you have an all-male panel!" Tumblr page that highlights panels, seminars, events, and various other things featuring male experts only.[9]

"It's the greatest website ever, [it] is awesome, it has like a David Hasselhoff-like icon. It says things like congratulations! Congratulations, you did it! You did it! You did it again!"

This was not the first time Dr Maeda had encountered a diversity imbalance. In his early days at RISD, according to Dr Maeda, about 70% of the student body was made up of women.

"I would be like, so where are the men?" says Dr Maeda.

To help to address the gender imbalance, scholarship programs were bolstered by developing a number of new relationships with organizations to enable students from historically underrepresented backgrounds to access art and design education. As well as taking steps to address the gender imbalance, in 2011, while Dr Maeda was president, RISDiversity was established to provide a platform for students and faculty to acknowledge and celebrate different viewpoints, work styles, and personalities. Dr Maeda says the initiative highlighted that no matter how individuals might represent or present themselves, everyone is different in some way, and it is the differences that we should be proud of and celebrate.

"It's a topic I have persisted with and remain passionate about," Dr Maeda says.[10]

He also mentioned a short animated film made by Pixar titled *Purl* that delivers a message about gender equality in the workplace that he feels is useful for men to watch. "Yeah, this is like a required thing, especially for males that have too much of a man-energy problem."[11]

Bringing design to a wider audience

Following his move to Silicon Valley, Dr Maeda has been featured in TED talks, current affairs TV programs, and industry interviews as a high-profile unofficial ambassador for design. Since 2015 (with one exception due to the COVID-19 pandemic), irrespective of the organization he was working for at the time, Dr Maeda has presented his annual *Design in Tech Report*[12] at the South by Southwest (SXSW) conference and exhibition, which takes place annually in mid-March in Austin, Texas. Established in 1987, SXSW claims to be the world's largest annual music, film, technology, and creative industries festival and conference of its kind.[13]

Inspired by KPCB partner Mary Meeker's widely followed annual *Internet Trends* reports, which document macro- and socioeconomic conditions, the financial markets, and the evolution of technologies, Dr Maeda's *Design in Tech Report* focused on the intersection of design and technology in the commercial world. Dr Maeda noted while Mary Meeker's *Internet Trends* would often refer to how the quality or experience of a product or service was a determining factor for business success, the word "design" was not explicitly used. Consequently, Dr Maeda saw an opportunity to clarify how design and designers play a fundamental role in business processes, especially in the technology industry.

When Dr Maeda presented his first *Design in Tech Report* at SXSW in 2015, the report was based on his first two years of observations and experiences while working in Silicon Valley, or as Dr Maeda terms the report, "a kind of music album of knowledge." Assisted by what he describes as "a team of curious, younger folks at KPCB" who helped to create the report, Dr Maeda explains he was seeking to reach a wider audience by connecting the worlds of design, technology, and business together instead of viewing the fields as three separate entities. The goal, he says, was to draw attention to the potential created when the productivities of design, technology, and business are strategically brought together.

Drawing on extensive research and conversations with designers, the *Design in Tech Report* focused on trends ranging from the then rising importance of design in the entrepreneurial ecosystem to venture capitalists funding start-ups that had designers as co-founders. The report highlighted how companies that bring design, technology, and business together were able to create new solutions for complex problems. It also covered trends ranging from the record amounts of funding flowing into design-led start-ups to merger and acquisition activities involving major tech corporations. As a result, Dr Maeda noted that design professionals were becoming more visible participants in management teams in Silicon Valley.[14]

While Dr Maeda's inaugural *Design in Tech Report* was intended to appeal to a broad audience, the response from some sections of the design community was distinctly lukewarm.

"There were designers that said it was poorly designed," Dr Maeda recalls. Comments were also made about a lack of "polish" and the dated slide format used, an allegation Dr Maeda does not dispute. However, Dr Maeda emphasizes the report was never intended to impress "just" the design community; it was meant to elevate the importance of design in the world of finance and business.[15]

With the *Design in Tech Report* available online, Dr Maeda and fellow KPCB partners Jackie Xu, Aviv Gilboa, and Justin Sayarath hoped that the presentation would attract a few thousand views. Instead, by the end of the year it had garnered more than 800,000 views. Ironically, while some in the design community had criticized the presentation, the *Design in Tech Report* made a list of "must-read SlideShares" in 2015.[16]

Building on the success of the 2015 *Design in Tech Report*, the 2016 and 2017 reports noted how the general word "design" would come to mean less as the use of technology rapidly grew, requiring more specific terms to qualify different types of design. Dr Maeda observed that when people talk about "design," they often make the mistake of not

*Dr Maeda presenting his first **Design in Tech Report** at SXSW in 2015*

differentiating between the different types of design and their applications. Believing the word "design" tended to have indistinct meanings for many business people, including those working in the design environment, Dr Maeda used his *Design in Tech Report* platform to introduce his own classification for three different types of design: classical design, design thinking, and computational design.

Classical design refers to a more traditional style taught in schools at the time and typically relates to the design of tangible objects and products; for example, shoes and furniture.

Design thinking, on the other hand, varies dramatically from classical design because it uses data and information—often related to customer needs—at the beginning of a project as a way to drive innovation and the business process. Meanwhile, computational design makes use of digital tools such as algorithms and data models to provide designers with more options to solve creative challenges and improve the overall product and brand experience. In his 2016 SXSW presentation, Dr Maeda explained the computational design system is not a replacement for designers, but augments the workflow in a way that a designer's time is spent reviewing and selecting the best creative choices to effectively speed up the design process and improve design efficiency. Dr Maeda also noted while business leaders were beginning to recognize the value of computational design through improved user experience, better products, and increased sales, many organizations were still struggling to put computational design into practice.[17]

Partly in response to feedback suggesting that previous *Design in Tech Reports* were too focused on the US, and in part because of emerging design influences from mainland China, the 2017 *Design in Tech Report* included a section on the mainland Chinese design landscape. The report highlighted design in tech principles and practices that had leapfrogged industry development cycles in the innovation and technology environment elsewhere in the world. For example, how the embedded WeChat QR code reader provided a frictionless method for interaction allowing the user to scan a QR code to make payments or visit a website. The report also highlighted how designers were among the co-founders of pioneering mainland Chinese companies, including two of Alibaba's co-founders and two of the eight Xiaomi co-founders.[18] The 2018 and 2019 *Design in Tech Reports* also noted how mainland China was rolling out design experiences at a scale and level of effectiveness that was breaking new ground.

In 2020, with SXSW cancelled due to the COVID-19 pandemic, Dr Maeda delivered his report findings as a YouTube webcast from his home studio. Renamed as the *CX Report* (with CX meaning "computational experience"), Dr Maeda introduced it as "a year's worth of thinking" and a "tool to put his thoughts in order." He focused his observations on business trends in the computational era by examining technologies for products and marketing in the context of digital transformation. Noting how he missed the interaction with the audience at SXSW, in what he announced was his first live home studio broadcast experiment, Dr Maeda explained how he had broadened the scope of the report to cover the larger surface of digital business transformation activities happening around the world. For example, the report explored why businesses at the organizational level should care holistically about the technology "experience." The report also delved into the biggest trends shaping the technology experience for established companies and the biggest changes in how tech and design had impacted the customer experience positively and negatively.[19]

The following year, again against the backdrop of the ongoing COVID-19 pandemic, the *CX Report* was titled *Safety Eats the World*, a play on engineer and investor Marc Andreessen's famous phrase from 2011 that "software is eating the world."[20] In the 2021 report, Dr Maeda focused on trends at the intersection of humanity, technology, and business. As companies and individuals were forced to adapt to remote working accelerated by the COVID-19 pandemic, Dr Maeda explored human safety and business resiliency through design and technology for both the private and public sectors. Noting how it is easy to confuse remote work with distributed work, Dr Maeda pointed out while remote work is procedural based and requires cooperation, distributed work entails a new way of corporate thinking based on collaboration. With this in mind, to achieve frictionless collaboration, Dr Maeda highlighted the growing availability of technologies that enable work to be done digitally in real time, such as live editing and simultaneous feedback. However, as digital and cloud-based collaboration tools continue to proliferate, Dr Maeda stressed that a company's ability to empower a distributed workforce depends on in-depth understanding of their business and operations capabilities as well as the needs and sentiments of their employees.[21]

In 2022, with the COVID-19 pandemic receding, yet against a backdrop of climate change, societal disruptions, and digital transformation, the report was renamed the *ResilienceTech Report*. Dr Maeda focused on the steady rise of technologies aimed at achieving greater personal, enterprise, and community resilience. Speaking at SXSW, Dr Maeda said the report was an attempt to push through the dark to find the light, taking into account the challenges and difficulties people around the world had been through during the previous couple of years. He added that, on a personal basis, he found by confronting things that made him feel uncomfortable or fearful, he tended to fear them less.[22]

Reverting to its original title *Design in Tech Report* with the subtitle *Design and Artificial Intelligence*, which acknowledged the rapid rise of pre-trained foundation models and so-called "large language model AI," in 2023 Dr Maeda highlighted the importance of not only advancing technology, but also cultivating a deeper understanding of the human experience. With more than 50 people from different industries and specializations contributing to the report, one of the main thrusts focused on the impact that AI in its various forms is having on the design industry as well as the wider business and social world. Setting aside some of the concerns associated with the proliferation of AI, Dr Maeda said in essence, AI should allow people to do more of the things they want to do and less of the things they do not want to do. At the same time as AI presents the game-changing potential to do things like improve efficiency, bring down costs, and accelerate research and development, Dr Maeda emphasized the importance of paying attention to design ethics, the elements of design that focus on people as people instead of as prospects or customers.

He also stressed the need to think critically when using voice prompts to interact with AI functions.

"It can be like trying to communicate with an alien," Dr Maeda said, citing the 2016 science fiction film *Arrival* as an example of communicating with an alien race within a set of limitations to discover the language of the alien through trial and error.[23]

As questions continue about whether AI is a friend or foe, Dr Maeda's 10th anniversary 2024 *Design in Tech Report* with the subtitle *Design Against AI* explored past and present inflection points between AI and design and the growing influence of AI in daily life. Pointing out there are a lot of unknowns relating to how AI will ultimately change the world of work, Dr Maeda suggested that understanding how computation works, which does not necessarily include coding, could help to make the AI landscape better for everyone. He added that he envisions design standing at that forefront of helping to articulate the value AI is able to create. When working with AI, Dr Maeda stressed the importance of providing large language models with context.

"If you don't give it context, it doesn't know anything. It's going to guess," he said during his presentation. "It's a new kind of technology. It's built out of math. It can do good things. It can do bad things. It's up to us humans who want to do good things with it to do better things for the world."[24]

An advocate for design

As someone who has held a prominent position in the design world for more than three decades, as an artist, designer, higher-education leader, and business executive who has shuttled between different industries, over the years Dr Maeda's views on design have both evolved and diversified.

As a speaker invited to make presentations all over the world, from Beijing to Davos to São Paulo to New York, Dr Maeda has spoken extensively about the intersection between art, design, technology, and business and provided insights on a wide range of design-related topics including creative leadership, inclusion, computation-led design, and more recently, design and AI. Shedding light on the respective approaches and purposes of design, Dr Maeda has described designers as problem solvers who analyze complex issues and employ their skills and expertise to develop purposeful solutions.[25] Along the way, he has made a number of memorable quotes such as, "Design is a solution to a problem. Art is a question to a problem,"[26] "Design is thinking made visual,"[27] and "The future of design lies in the combination of human empathy and computer intelligence."[28]

Dr Maeda's *Design in Tech Reports* are considered by many as providing a wide lens on design topics that matter for businesses. As an author, the six books written by Dr Maeda including *How to Speak Machine: Computational Thinking for the*

Rest of Us, *The Laws of Simplicity,* and *Redesigning Leadership* have sought to reach an audience beyond the design profession.

From his early days of working in Silicon Valley, foretelling an inflection point when the distinction between coding and design would become less defined, to help designers gain fresh perspectives, Dr Maeda has encouraged them to work with people who are different from themselves. At the same time, to further strengthen the design profession's value proposition, he encourages designers to take a deeper interest in business processes. From the time he was a professor at MIT, Dr Maeda has advocated for coders and designers to become more aware of each other's disciplines, a coming together he neatly termed as "coders who can design and designers who can code." Dr Maeda recalls when he first raised the concept, it was at a time when the idea of combining design and technology was for the most part unexplored, which led to some unfavorable responses, notably from the classical fields of art and design.[29]

This was not to be the first or the last time during his multifaceted career that Dr Maeda attracted criticism from professionals within the design community. In 2019 Dr Maeda was quoted in an article published by *Fast Company* with a headline which read, "In reality, design is not that important,"[30] which triggered a backlash of comments.

"Boy, did people hate me for saying that," Dr Maeda says, noting that the "clickbait headline" still provokes a reaction when people discover it on the internet. "People say, like,

I can't believe you said that. Do you know how hard it is to be a designer in a company and not be considered as being anything?"

Explaining how the quote was taken out of context from a telephone interview that covered a wide range of design-related topics, Dr Maeda says the point he was intending to make was instead of debating whether design has enough influence over a product or status within an organization, designers should focus on being part of a team with the shared vision of making products and services that solve people's problems. Whether it is labeled as design-led, product-led, marketing-led, or engineering-led, Dr Maeda believes that ultimately it is teamwork which is the most important.

In hindsight, Dr Maeda says while his comment could be considered as not giving due recognition to the design profession, it was an example of the way a remark or observation can be misconstrued by the media. Nevertheless, he knows the response to the *Fast Company* headline provided useful feedback.

"I'm a big believer in user research. It's a good way of collecting data and helps me to improve," says Dr Maeda. That said, Dr Maeda explains that one of the reasons he is a prolific user of social media platforms is because they enable him to discuss design and other topics and use his own words "to think out loud" instead of leaving it to someone else to interpret what he says.[31]

More recently, Dr Maeda has been turning his attention to the intersection of design and AI. During a Microsoft WorkLab podcast interview with Elise Hu, Dr Maeda said design today is going to play an important role in the large language model AI world with a perspective on ethics.[32] With trust as a key factor, Dr Maeda explained the type of trust which previously could be found embedded in great products will now have to be better than ever when it comes to products designed using AI tools. For example, it will not be enough for a product to be functional and aesthetically pleasing.

"It's not just the aesthetics, the beauty, but the aesthetics of the ethics inside any experience user's encounter," Dr Maeda explained. Or, as Dr Maeda has said on a number of occasions, technology, in this case AI, makes possibilities, while design makes solutions.

05

Beyond
Silicon Valley

A wider landscape to integrate design and technology

In 2016, three years after he became the first design partner at venture capital firm KPCB, invigorated by what he described on LinkedIn as his "post-doc" Silicon Valley experiences, Dr Maeda joined the online publishing company Automattic—the parent company of WordPress and a number of other tech platforms—as Global Head of Computational Design and Inclusion.[1] To ensure he stayed in touch with the Silicon Valley design evolution environment, Dr Maeda retained an open-ended arrangement as a strategic advisor to KPCB.

Established in 2005 as a role model and innovator in remote work, also known as fully distributed work, Automattic's headquarters are located in San Francisco. At the time Dr Maeda joined, Automattic's close to 500 staff, known as "Automatticians," were spread across more than 50 countries. Long before remote working practices were accelerated by the COVID-19 pandemic, Automattic's entire workforce worked from home, or more precisely, from wherever in the world they chose to work. Instead of living in Airbnb accommodation, for the first time in a number of years Dr Maeda was able to live with his family in Lexington, Massachusetts. However, while

Dr Maeda valued the opportunity to be closer to his family, especially his two youngest daughters, focusing on work commitments meant he was unable to spend as much time with them as he would have liked.

"When you are working at a computer all the time you are not really at home, as people found out during the COVID pandemic," Dr Maeda explains. "Success is terribly imperfect; it's not like the movies where people have a perfect work-life balance."[2]

In his new role at Automattic, instead of advising start-ups, CEOs, and design leaders as he did at KPCB, through his interdisciplinary approach to design and technology, Dr Maeda was tasked with integrating design and technology practices into Automattic's design team workflow. As a platform to showcase design work and promote inclusion among the company's design team, soon after joining Automattic, Dr Maeda launched a site called Design.blog (which is no longer online). Acting as the editor, Dr Maeda compiled the how and why of Automattic's design projects to identify common threads and synthesize them into principles and best practices. The distillation of the work the design team produced brought more people into the process, which Dr Maeda believed was preferable to proposing ideas he thought could work. The concept of Automattic's design team sharing insights and best practices resonated strongly with Dr Maeda's interest in inclusion, as did the company's creed, "I will never stop learning." With this in mind, in 2018, Dr Maeda was instrumental in launching the Automattic Design Award, which served to showcase the work of the design community within the WordPress ecosystem.[3] However, the awards scheme was discontinued when Dr Maeda left the company.

Eager to continue his efforts to expand inclusion, a passion that began when he was a professor at MIT, when he joined Automattic Dr Maeda requested that "inclusion" be part of his title. This led to some people mistakenly assuming he had joined the human resources field, a profession Dr Maeda holds in high regard.

"Putting inclusion in my title was a mistake, but a mistake that I was glad about because I was so passionate about this stuff," Dr Maeda explains.

Inclusivity can be a tough topic to broach because everyone is different. Nevertheless, Dr Maeda says that adding "inclusion" to his title provided him with a consistent reminder to hold himself to a higher standard. For example, in addition to considering gender, ethnicity, race, and people living with disabilities, being aware that inclusion and diversity can be influenced by geographic, cultural, and socioeconomic status. Making no claims that he has been able to maintain a perfect record for inclusion and diversity, Dr Maeda says he continually strives to heighten his awareness. During meetings and interviews, he is conscious about his choice of words and the phrases he uses. For example, using the word "wild" instead of saying "crazy" because of the potential negative inference to mental health problems. He also ensures he keeps up to date with orientations and identities added to the LGBTQ (lesbian, gay, bisexual, transgender, and queer) acronym, such as A (asexual).

However, in spite of Dr Maeda's best intentions to maintain a high standard of inclusion awareness, there have been occasions when his efforts have fallen short of others' expectations. Dr Maeda recalls being a guest speaker at a technology event, when as he was about to begin his presentation, a member of the audience approached him on stage to raise an issue about the accessibility of a web application.

"She came at me pointing her phone and asking me to explain why a particular feature that was related to inclusion wasn't accessible," Dr Maeda says.

While the unexpected encounter was slightly scary, it reinforced how important inclusion, in all of its various forms, really is.

Both conscious and curious about the way that the WordPress open-source platform provided the opportunity for anyone to create and share content, Dr Maeda's new position placed him at the forefront of improving the user experience where he focused on enriching the system with diverse options and tools to reach the broadest range of users possible. As an example, Dr Maeda spearheaded a project to introduce students in Paintsville, Kentucky, located in Appalachia coal country, to design as a career path while also showing them the possibilities of remote work. To learn about jobs in design, through the internet, students were able to interview well-known designers as well as Automattic designers. The idea for the project, named A3 (Appalachia, AGI, Automattic), was sparked when Dr Maeda joined former Chief Technology Officer of the United States Megan Smith on a Tech Jobs Tour which was designed to bring technical jobs to the country outside of the US coastal areas.[4]

To learn about the environment the students lived in, Dr Maeda visited Paintsville on the Tech Jobs Tour initiative. When asked if he had read J. D. Vance's bestselling *Hillbilly Elegy* about Appalachian values, Dr Maeda was able to answer that it was after reading the book he was inspired to visit Appalachia, which had helped him to check his preconceptions and form his own opinions. It was only when Dr Maeda travelled to Paintsville he discovered the area was famous for being visited by US President Lyndon Baines Johnson, often referred to as L. B. J., in the 1960s, as representing one of the poorest parts of the United States.[5] Dr Maeda also spent time in Detroit with African-American business owners to learn about their challenges and ambitions. By visiting places that often had limited access to computers and by working with the local people, Dr Maeda explains he was able to develop a better understanding of specific needs and ways that Automattic's technology products could provide useful benefits.[6]

Dr Maeda presenting as part of Tech Jobs Tour 2017

During his three-year tenure with Automattic, Dr Maeda also continued to present his annual *Design in Tech Reports* at SXSW (see chapter 4). In addition to providing a timely focus on the ever-changing world of design and tech, reflecting his work at Automattic, in his annual *Design in Tech Report* presentations Dr Maeda included examples of why design and inclusion are inseparable, and why design that incorporates inclusiveness is good for business. While designers in general tend to be welcoming of diversity and inclusiveness, Dr Maeda pointed out there was a tendency for designers with similar upbringings and social circles to design for people within similar parameters. A solution, he suggested, was for designers to interact with and learn from people who are not like themselves, and by working with them, design products for a broader group of people.

Providing clarity in the digital age

In 2019, Dr Maeda's sixth book was published in the US as *How to Speak Machine: Computational Thinking for the Rest of Us* (Penguin Random House) and *How to Speak Machine: Laws of Design for a Digital Age* in the UK and elsewhere. Although it was still the pre-ChatGPT era, AI in different forms was being increasingly integrated into business and consumer applications.

With much of the content of his book based on research findings related to his annual *Design in Tech Reports*, Dr Maeda says that writing *How to Speak Machine* provided a way to frame his thoughts and observations, or as Dr Maeda puts it, place some context around the invisible world of AI and machine learning which he defines as "large language models that behave like an indefatigable living organism that can span infinite space, focus on infinitesimally fine detail, and never get tired or need to take a break."

"The machine language is the language of an invisible world that connects all of us together," Dr Maeda says.

In an age when computational power is growing exponentially, characterized by AI devices equipped with the capability to communicate with humans, the ability to speak both machine and human can be an advantage and help to build resilience in an increasingly technology-driven world.

With six chapters that focus on what computation was, is, and is becoming, Dr Maeda explains that *How to Speak Machine* aims to help non-tech people move beyond the myths of AI and machine learning, to gain a better understanding of the various strengths and weaknesses.

"I saw so many people being left behind," Dr Maeda says, adding that it can be difficult for those not trained in computer science to understand the impact computation can have.

A prime example was the way that machine learning, one of the most common types of AI which is primarily used to process large amounts of data quickly, was emerging across areas of business and industries where traditionally people had limited connections with technology. Dr Maeda also notes while human relationships with digital devices were changing, outside of people with an understanding of computer science, generally there was a thin grasp of how the underlying technologies operated. In some cases, people using natural language prompts to connect with their devices humanized their interactions in the belief there was a "real person" behind the technology.

Using easy-to-understand explanations, *How to Speak Machine* provides a layperson's perspective of fundamental computing concepts such as processing loops, recursion, and neural networks. Drawing attention to Moore's law, a computing term that has been used since the 1970s which states the processing power of computers doubles every two years, *How to Speak Machine* explains different ways the evolving field of AI expands the accessibility and the scope with which technology tools can be applied. *How to Speak Machine* also includes autobiographical elements from Dr Maeda's hands-on experiences with technology, design, and business that add a wide range of perspectives to the different ways that computation is transforming the design of products and services alongside numerous aspects of daily life.

At the time of writing *How to Speak Machine,* many doubted that Dr Maeda's insights would come to fruition.

"People were like, no way, that's not possible. Computers are not gonna embody living behavior, it will never happen," says Dr Maeda. "I was like, 'Oh, okay'."[7]

In his review of *How to Speak Machine* on Amazon, Douglas Rushkoff, documentarian and author of 20 books including *Team Human*, wrote, "John Maeda engineers rapprochement between humans and our computational creations in this engaging, enlightening book."[8]

Meanwhile, on the Barnes and Noble website, Jake Knapp, *New York Times* bestselling author of *Sprint*, declared, *"How to Speak Machine* is like nothing I've ever read. It will rewire your brain (in a good way). A must-read for anyone looking to shape the future."

Also on the Barnes and Noble website, Emily Chang, Bloomberg TV host and bestselling author of *Brotopi*, wrote, "Riveting and important. A book with as much to teach about human behavior as it does technology."[9]

While *How to Speak Machine* was written at a time when AI was on the cusp of becoming a "hot topic," Dr Maeda believes his book was published too soon, four years before the AI phenomenon became part of mainstream society. "It was a timing thing. Sometimes you get it right, sometimes you don't," he says.[10]

Delivering design practices at scale

In a video he filmed with Cannes, France in the background in June 2019,[11] Dr Maeda announced he had joined Publicis Sapient, the digital business transformation hub of French advertising conglomerate Publicis Groupe, as the company's Chief Experience Officer. During the period he worked for Publicis Sapient, while Dr Maeda was mainly based in Massachusetts, when necessary, he traveled to France as well as other countries.

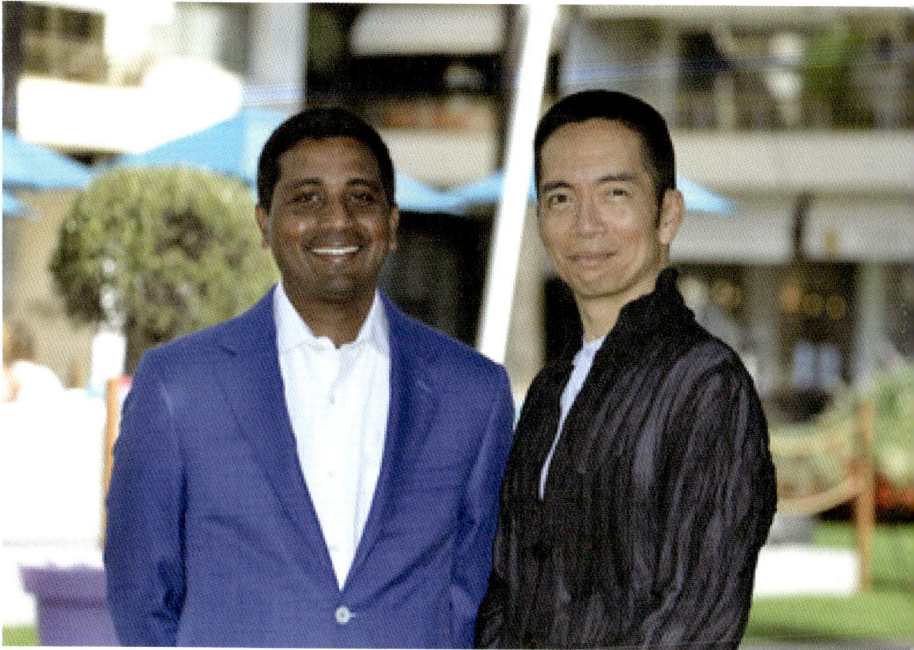

Dr Maeda and Publicis Sapient CEO Nigel Vaz in Cannes

Outlining details of his new role, Dr Maeda explained that joining one of the world's largest technology consulting companies would enable him to introduce computational design practices to the Publicis Groupe and the company's customers, at a scale he could never have imagined.

The difference between Dr Maeda's new role and his responsibilities at Automattic, where he had mainly focused on digital products and design, would involve connecting multiple areas including product, engineering, marketing, IT, and C-suite. This would include working with some of the largest companies in the world, including well-established traditional companies that were facing challenges from technology companies that had become global digital giants. The aim, Dr Maeda explained, was to combine what traditional companies had always done well with the technology and culture of a start-up. Speaking on the CodeNewbie podcast soon after he joined Publicis Sapient, Dr Maeda said it was as if he had moved from the vegetable section of a supermarket to working across the entire supermarket, including pushing shopping carts around the parking lot.[12]

Joining Publicis Sapient also involved Dr Maeda making a professional adjustment of another type. Prior to joining Publicis Sapient, Dr Maeda had served on the boards of directors for wireless hi-fi innovator Sonos and the global advertising firm Wieden+Kennedy. However, due to conflicts of interest, he was required to resign. Dr Maeda explains that when he served on company boards he viewed his main role to be an advocate for diversity.

"I was like the diversity person. I never fitted any kind of typical legal or pure business background, which is common. I was someone who could bring a different opinion to a board." Dr Maeda says in addition to bringing the contribution and value of creative teams to the attention of board members, as a board member himself he learned how boards play a key role in balancing innovation with continuity.

"They're there to stabilize, so over time my interest became more of a stabilizer versus divergence." Dr Maeda says that, given his background, he was also adept at helping company boards handle a crisis.

"I'm not saying I wanted to see more crises, but I love crisis management. It's sort of my sweet spot. Oh, a crisis, no problem, let me work on that one." Dr Maeda says it was handling crises that drew him to the resilience technology field later in life.[13]

Although Dr Maeda only stayed with Publicis Sapient for a little over a year, he was able to make an impact working with fellow Silicon Valley recruits: Wendy Johansson, Global Vice President of Experience Transformation, and Leah Buley, Group Vice President, Experience Research Lead. Together they rebuilt the way that Publicis Sapient delivered experience outcomes. Notably, the rebuild included a system by which Publicis Sapient's creative talent could be managed by skills instead of titles. With a wide spectrum of design talent to draw upon, the goal was to address the challenge of differentiating between design talent that mainly worked on decorations or aesthetics and design talent that dealt with solving design problems at scale.

Powered by computation, to match talent to projects and also to support talent development, Dr Maeda and his team created an in-house categorization system managed by Publicis Sapient's cloud-based LEAD (light, ethical, accessible, dataful) system. Equally notable was the reshaping of the model of delivery from "billable people" to "winner-doers" which, according to a LinkedIn post,[14] grew the direct margin during the peak of COVID-19's economic impact. With both Dr Maeda and Wendy Johansson familiar with the operational structure of all-distributed global workplaces, by early August 2019, they had moved Publicis Sapient's entire Experience team to the distributed work environment. With approximately 1,000 Experience team members digitally connected across 30 offices, when the ramifications of COVID-19 hit hard six months later in early 2020, the strategic initiative proved to be invaluable.

On a personal level, Dr Maeda's thoughts were turning to another matter, the issue of succession or, more specifically, making room for the next generation of leadership within Publicis Sapient's Experience team. With the Experience team having adopted the Rooney rule[15] for the succession planning of leaders, it meant that on every list of potential successors to any leader there needed to be at least one woman or underrepresented minority. Adopted in 2003 as a model for boosting diversity and inclusion by the National Football League (NFL), one of the major professional sports leagues in the United States and Canada, the Rooney rule was created in response to Tampa's firing of then Head Coach Tony Dungy, despite a winning record. The Rooney rule sought to address the issue of the imbalance of diversity in the league, where about 70% of the players were minorities, but few held leadership positions.

With talent in the pipeline clearly prepared and ready for more challenges and opportunities, Dr Maeda decided it was time to step aside. In a LinkedIn post[16] explaining why he left Publicis Sapient, Dr Maeda wrote, "'Am I an impediment to their future progression? Shouldn't I, too, #MakeRoom for them?' So I decided to do so."

A fulfilling mission

In October 2020, with the COVID-19 pandemic severely disrupting virtually all aspects of business and daily life, Dr Maeda joined Boston-based Everbridge, a provider of critical event management (CEM), as the company's Chief Customer Experience Officer. Founded in the aftermath of 9/11, under the banner of "Keep People Safe and Businesses Running," Everbridge's CEM solutions are geared towards a wide range of critical events including terrorist attacks and severe weather conditions, as well as critical business events including IT outages, cyberattacks, or other incidents such as product recalls or supply-chain interruptions.

In his new role, Dr Maeda led Everbridge's technology and product vision for enabling resilience at the company, city, and country levels with a focus on large language models (AI/machine learning) and outcomes-driven approaches to visualization. Explaining his role in more detail,[17] Dr Maeda said his core priority was to ensure the company's technologies and products delivered an experience that made it easier for customers to keep their people safe and their organizations running. In effect, he said, this meant utilizing technology to deliver products that meet users' increasingly complex enterprise software experience expectations. Dr Maeda explained that depending on whether the user is a novice or an expert, the enterprise software user experience can vary. He also pointed out that, in a relatively short time span mobile devices and larger screens had extensively evolved, which had changed the way that individuals responsible for safety and keeping businesses running interacted with enterprise software. "It's no longer the case of the user adapting to the software; the software needs to adapt to the user's expected experience." Dr Maeda noted how this required a new approach to delivering positive user experiences, which could be achieved through design and technology.

In a press release, Everbridge welcomed Dr Maeda with a glowing endorsement which described him as "bringing unmatched credentials" to the company, adding that, "as a renowned technologist and designer, Dr Maeda would help innovate the next generation of critical event management for every stakeholder in a world where safety and resiliency standards are forever changed by the coronavirus pandemic."[18]

Personally, at a time when the stakes of managing critical events well and more proactively had rarely been higher, due to the coronavirus, Dr Maeda said he was excited to apply his experience to digitally transform how organizations communicate and solve business problems in this incredibly important area. He added that Everbridge offered a platform where he could have the most impact in helping to save lives and livelihoods, which he described as a "truly fulfilling mission."[19] However, in spite of service engagements spanning tens of thousands of projects in over 150 countries and facilitating tens of billions of critical interactions, Dr Maeda admitted he was unaware of Everbridge's existence until shortly before he joined the company.

"Everbridge is the ubiquitous company that you've never heard about," Dr Maeda wrote on LinkedIn.[20]

Quickly up to speed with the services Everbridge offered, Dr Maeda took his mission to share his insights on ways to tackle critical events through technology and design—such as the outbreak of the global coronavirus pandemic to extreme weather events, cyberattacks, and business disruptions—to a wider audience, including participating in high-profile events. For example, in 2020 he was a keynote speaker at Everbridge's "COVID-19 R2R: The Road to Recovery" virtual leadership summit, which also featured George W. Bush, the 43rd president of the United States, as well as presidential advisor and Director of the National Institute of Allergy and Infectious Diseases at the US National Institutes of Health Dr Anthony Fauci, Virgin Group founder Sir Richard Branson, and renowned neurosurgeon and CNN Chief Medical Correspondent Dr Sanjay Gupta.[21] Recognizing the importance of CEM amid the

COVID-19 pandemic, Dr Maeda was ranked 11th on a 2020 list of top influencers on LinkedIn, joining well-known individuals including Melinda Gates, Mark Cuban, and David Solomon, CEO of Goldman Sachs.[22]

As he had done since 2015, while at Everbridge, Dr Maeda shaped his annual *Design in Tech Reports* around current events pertinent to the intersection of design, technology, and business. As exemplified by the COVID-19 pandemic and ensuing vaccine dissemination challenges, in 2021 Dr Maeda noted that, with a new critical event seemingly emerging every day of the week, the science of effectively managing them, or mismanaging them, was front page news. With this in mind, the 2021 *Design in Tech Report* (renamed the *CX Report*) highlighted safety technology as a key factor for accelerating digital transformation during and after the pandemic.[23]

Dr Maeda also found his own way to navigate COVID-19 restrictions. Frustrated by not being able to travel as frequently as he would have liked and finding it difficult to apply the concentration needed to work from home, he discovered there was an empty office building not too far from where he lived, which he was able to use for work purposes.

"It was great, because I was able to go to work," he says, noting that it felt comfortable to separate work from home life.[24]

Dr Maeda remained with Everbridge until October 2022. In a post on LinkedIn which received more than 110 comments and over 840 reactions,[25] he announced he was returning to his birthplace of Seattle, to join Microsoft as Vice President of Engineering, Head of Computational Design / AI Platform. Similar to previous occasions when he has sought new learning experiences, Dr Maeda felt his move to Microsoft took place at a time when the AI "surf is rising," which aligned with his sense of curiosity.

"I want to see how lucky I will get," he says.

An area of AI that currently excites him is multimodal AI, which combines multiple types, or modes, of data to accurately create interpretations of still images, video, and audio. "Oh my gosh, it's amazing."

Dr Maeda explains that multimodal AI allows a user to point a camera at any subject and the system will interpret the image into any language. "It's an incredible breakthrough for the unsighted and vision impaired."[26]

When Dr Maeda joined Microsoft in November 2022, it was not the first time he had come close to working for the tech giant. As a teenager living in Seattle, Dr Maeda applied for an internship with Microsoft. However, he failed what was known as the "operator precedence rules in C" test, a practical proficiency test computer engineers take during the recruitment process.

"I told the interviewer that I could type fast enough to elicit the correct combination, so it wasn't a big deal," Dr Maeda disclosed in a LinkedIn post written in 2023. Dr Maeda explained to the interviewer he was unable to complete the operator precedence test in one attempt and always did it iteratively, but the interviewer did not believe him.

At the time dyslexia was not as well recognized or understood as it is today, which could have explained Dr Maeda's propensity for reversing the sequences of words and objects. This time, Dr Maeda quipped, he was not tested on operator precedence rules in C. But just in case the interviewer from his past shows up somewhere on the Microsoft premises, he has his operator precedence chart cheat sheet in his wallet. Importantly, Dr Maeda joined Microsoft at a time when the company is fully open to, and inclusive of, the full spectrum of neurodiversity.[27]

Unraveling artificial intelligence

Artificial intelligence (AI) may seem like a fairly recent phenomenon, but Dr Maeda first encountered it in the 1980s as an undergraduate at MIT. For more than three decades as an academic, designer, and business executive, he has had a front-row seat as AI has transcended from the realm of mainly science fiction to mainstream use.

Since 2015 when he presented his first *Design in Tech Report* at SXSW, Dr Maeda has focused on tracking the evolution of AI and the implications for design and work in general, while raising fundamental questions about ethics and demystifying many of the features of AI and its uses. As an expert on the forefront of AI development, Dr Maeda has used the SXSW platform to share insights for entrepreneurs about how to engage with the new technology, the potential for AI to help leaders make better decisions, and his optimistic view on what the future holds for designers who embrace AI tools.

At the 2024 SXSW, Dr Maeda noted, while some people refer to advancements being like a "summer for AI," from his perspective, it is still early springtime and the current uses of AI are only at the tip of the iceberg of what is possible. "There is so much to figure out," he said.[28]

As an undergraduate, Dr Maeda took an artificial intelligence course with Dr Joseph Weizenbaum, the inventor of the ELIZA program, which simulated conversation by using pattern matching language and was the predecessor to chatbots today. Even though Dr Weizenbaum was responsible for inventing the forerunner of today's chatbots, he became an outspoken critic of the potential misuse of and overdependence on powerful computers.[29] Not giving much thought to Dr Weizenbaum's achievements, like many students of his age, Dr Maeda dismissed him "as being just another professor."

Several decades later, Dr Maeda has a newfound respect for his former professor. In particular, he has been drawn to statements Dr Weizenbaum made in his book *Computer Power and Human Reason: From Judgment to Calculation* including, "the question is not whether such a thing *can* be done, but whether it is appropriate to delegate this hitherto human function to a machine" and "since we do not now have any ways of making computers wise, we ought not now to give computers tasks that demand wisdom."[30]

During the course of his multidimensional career, Dr Maeda has experienced firsthand the various ebbs and flows of AI development. The time when he was a student at MIT in the 1980s coincided with a period when enthusiasm for AI was cooling down, mainly due to the challenge of making innovations scalable and the realization that building AI tools was more complex than expected. Compounding the issue was the amount of computing power and data required to enable algorithms to function. Towards the end of the 1980s and early 1990s, with advancements in computing power, interest in AI started to pick up again. When Dr Maeda returned to MIT as a professor at the MIT Media Lab in 1996, his team used a type of AI to sift through media information for the projects they were working on. Fast forward to today and Dr Maeda says he is surprised by how far AI has come.

"When we were using AI in the lab, I remember that no one thought it could do what it does today," Dr Maeda recalls.

At a point in time when humans are able to give machines natural language prompts, Dr Maeda believes that many of the growing number of "AI doomsday fears" can be mitigated with a better understanding of the way that AI works.

"It is important to understand what is going on underneath and in the background," he says. "When you understand how the machine really works, you're gonna fear it less."[31]

How large language models operate

Drawing on his experience as a graphic designer, visual artist, computer scientist, and business executive, Dr Maeda says a common misconception is to believe that AI tools can do everything, especially generative AI which is capable of creating text, images, and video. AI is seemingly everywhere and all at once, on the surface, while LLMs such as ChatGPT can give the sense of behaving similar to "people like us." But Dr Maeda notes it has become common, especially for people from a non-computer background, to perceive LLMs as being intelligent because they have the capability to learn and make human-like decisions based on the information they have access to. However, while LLMs have the ability to recognize and process information in a seemingly intelligent format, the interpretation of information is decidedly different from human intelligence.

Using a metaphor first coined by Herbert Simon, an American scientist and renowned AI pioneer, to demonstrate how LLMs operate like a pair of scissors, Dr Maeda says one blade of the scissors acts as the cognition model while the other blade is the context model.

"That's what's happening with the last generation of LLMs," Dr Maeda explains.

A computation model (cognition) is able to generate a sentence, but without any context. Meanwhile, the context model can search through unstructured data and find similar things that match the topic. For example, if a LLM is provided with a favorite food item it can search through unstructured data and find similar things that match the favorite food such as restaurants that serve the food, recipes, and the history of the food.

"This amazing new cognition blade has arrived, and now we can rub context against it and when you slice, slice, slice the two blades together, it creates what feels like intelligence."

Using the scissors concept to illustrate a hypothetical AI conversation, Dr Maeda suggests to imagine two people who do not know each other meeting for the first time and one person saying, "I think you like strawberry ice cream?"

The second person replies, "You know, I'm allergic to strawberries." This now constitutes context and the conversation continues with, "What do you like?"

"Well, I like chocolate ice cream."

"Why is that?"

"Because I grew up in a part of the world where chocolate was plentiful."

Now the context blade is getting longer so the next response could be, "Let's go to a restaurant that serves food from Madagascar."[32] While Madagascar grows less than 1% of the world's cacao, which chocolate is made from, Madagascar's cacao is known amongst chocolatiers and master chefs to be some of the best in the world.[33]

Will AI replace the need for human skills?

In terms of worker displacement or AI tools replacing jobs currently performed by humans, Dr Maeda points out that throughout history, at various times and in various forms, technology has replaced humans. For example, the way that ATMs replaced or reduced the need for bank cashiers and in more recent times, customer support lines that use chatbots to answer customer enquiries. The question that needs to be asked, Dr Maeda says, is what are the best ways that humans can utilize AI and shape its use to their advantage? For instance, AI tools are capable of doing work that people do not want to do, such as repetitive tasks. In theory, this could allow humans to spend more time doing the things they prefer to do. AI can also be a useful tool for those that have time constraints or need to multitask and cover numerous topics at the same time.

To better understand AI tools, Dr Maeda suggests learning how prompts work, learning how context works, and what it can and cannot be used for, while also being aware of the pros and cons. Reassuringly, he notes, if humans continue to be innovative, curious, and expand their own capabilities, they will never become completely expendable.

"This is what makes humans difficult to replace," Dr Maeda says. Instead of fearing AI, people could consider trying out various ways AI tools work.[34]

Cozy Kitchen

As the capabilities of AI and large language models like ChatGPT continue to advance, in 2023 Dr Maeda launched a series of programs on YouTube aimed at introducing a wider audience to AI. It is titled Mr (not Dr) Maeda's Cozy AI Kitchen, in part an homage to his youth growing up in the family-owned Star Tofu Manufacturing Company in Seattle, and in part designed to make AI more understandable. Each episode uses food and food containers to symbolize different elements of AI, where Dr Maeda produces a code recipe so that viewers can "cook" AI at home.[35] Similar to the way Dr Maeda's mother would put photographs of cooking with tofu on the wall of the tofu store to educate customers, in each episode Dr Maeda, wearing a cook's uniform and usually accompanied by an expert from a different technology discipline, provides insights and practical tips.

"I'm trying to put AI in the hands of more design and product decision makers, so it's less alienating to them," Dr Maeda explains.[36]

While the Cozy Kitchen videos are produced separately from Dr Maeda's role as Vice President of Engineering, Head of Computational Design / AI Platform at Microsoft, in several episodes he introduced Semantic Kernel, a recently launched Microsoft open-source software program that enables app developers and people who build enterprise applications—but may not be familiar with AI tools—to integrate AI into their developer tool kits.[37] With the true essence of Semantic Kernel easy to grasp, Dr Maeda says the primary goal is to empower developers to leverage the potential of AI.

"My big takeaway from working on [Semantic Kernel] has been this wonderful phrase that I think is gonna help a lot. It's called collaborative UX," says Dr Maeda, referring to the term used to describe the collaboration between humans and AI in the design and development process.[38]

A personal perspective

Confessing to being addicted to his digital devices, Dr Maeda notes that while many people have an emotional relationship with machines—their phone, computer, TikTok account—to the point where they are beholden to them and what they can do, he is the pilot and gives instructions to his devices which he mainly uses for timers and reminders. As someone who lives with dyslexia, is neuroatypical, and high on the autism spectrum, Dr Maeda finds generative AI useful for helping him to formulate his thoughts, which is particularly beneficial when generating a workflow process.

Explaining that he would not use generative AI to write a book because it would deprive him of the learning process, Dr

Maeda says generative AI is a beneficial tool for someone like himself who tends to be disorganized. However, he adds, it is important to give AI systems smart goals.

"You have to be a good boss," he says.[39]

Returning home

Returning to his birthplace and where he grew up has also prompted Dr Maeda to reappraise his perceptions of Seattle. As a youth it seemed it was raining and the city shrouded in fog. Other places Dr Maeda later lived in, like Cambridge, Dallas–Fort Worth, Yokohama, Tsukuba, Providence, and Palo Alto, always seemed to have bluer skies. Now that Dr Maeda is living in Seattle and able to compare the skies he has seen around the world, he is not so sure.[40]

Besides joining Microsoft, November 2022 was significant for Dr Maeda for another reason. Early in the month he travelled to Hong Kong to receive an honorary doctorate from the City University of Hong Kong (CityUHK) in recognition of his significant contributions to education and the well-being of society. Unfortunately, at the time of his visit, Hong Kong was subject to strict COVID-19 restrictions, which meant that Dr Maeda spent the majority of his time in his hotel room.[41]

However, this did not prevent him from drawing attention to CityUHK and Hong Kong's unique strengths and qualities in his acceptance address. Having lived most of his life at the intersection of worlds, Dr Madea explained, he had had the opportunity to see and bridge different points of view. He also shared his belief that Hong Kong was a "Type O" community of ever-expanding intersectionalities.

"The fact that Hong Kong has retained the ability to function so well over many decades is a testament to its first-rate intelligence as embodied by the faculty, staff and students at City University of Hong Kong," Dr Maeda said.[42]

As well as being able to spend time taking care of his aging parents, moving back to Seattle has enabled him to see more of his sister and his daughters that live in the area. Becoming a grandfather in 2022 also added a new dimension to Dr Maeda's life.

"As a family we have been able to spend more time together than we have done for many years." Dr Maeda explains that for much of his career, because of his work commitments, the places he lived away from his family he called home, yet were not home.

"I had a family, but I didn't have a family life," Dr Maeda adds.

In retrospect, while his family is aware that the sacrifices he made were for their benefit, he feels he could have done more to include his family in his work.

"When you feel that everything is counting on you, you are not so aware your family is part of the fulfilment equation," Dr Maeda says.

Reflecting on some of the compromises he has made because of his career choices, he notes there are feelings he has become more aware of later in life that he wished he had acknowledged earlier. He says it reminds him of the words written by Lebanese American writer and poet Kahlil Gibran, "When you are joyous, look deep into your heart and you shall find it is only that which has given you sorrow that is giving you joy."[43] Believing that life is a series of edits consisting of the ongoing process of refining and honing choices, decisions, and actions, by starting a new chapter in his career and spending more time with his family, Dr Maeda feels he has made a new beginning.

"2023 was an exceptionally good year," he says.[44]

Appendix:
Creative Leadership
Blog Posts

Father as Leader

First published online on 16 April 2011

I have regular open office hours for students—a practice that is often suggested for college presidents and for other leaders—the so-called "open door" philosophy. You learn all kinds of things about your organization when you do so.

A senior came to visit me, and often as seniors do, he spoke about his own wonderings as to what he would / could / should do after graduating. And this student was fairly at peace with the mystery and challenges ahead, as was evident in the fact that he didn't ask me any career questions. Instead he asked me an odd and interesting question that took me off guard: "In your role as a leader, how has being a father influenced how you lead?"

My response began from where I often stand—that children will inherit a world that you will either make better or worse for their adult lives. We all want better lives for all the future adults so we work in the present to improve the coming world to our best abilities. And we often fall short of success because, well, we are human. But we remind ourselves again to care, and to try again. And that's whether you are a parent or not—a better world is universally desirable.

I knew that wasn't really a response to his question, so I tried again. I spoke instead about my own father and how he influenced me as a leader. My father was a cook for many years. He left home (a small fishing village in Japan) at 15 and shined shoes on a boat for passengers as his first job in addition to cleaning the bathrooms and floors. On that boat he did every manner of job, and worked his way up to peeling potatoes in the kitchen, and then finally to becoming the cook of the ship. In the 60s he left the ship, and worked as a cook in a Japanese restaurant in Seattle; a decade later he took over a mom-and-pop tofu-making business and ended his career as a cook.

However Dad stayed active in his cooking craft; he loved to cook for guests at our house. It wasn't often, but when we would have guests come over he would get a whole fish and cut it as sashimi (raw fish) and arrange all the foods in beautiful ways. In many ways he was my first design teacher with his mastery in meticulously arranging the shapes, proportions, mixtures, selection of plates, and overall visual / textural / temperature balance of a multi-course traditional Japanese-style meal.

One day when I was about 11 or 12, I noted to my father his consistent pattern in how he would give the best parts of the fish to the guests, and for himself eat the scrappiest, undesirable parts. I thought this strange because as a cook he knew what tasted good and bad, so with his more developed taste acuities he should be eating the good parts himself. He plainly explained that a cook doesn't make food for himself to enjoy—he makes food for others to enjoy. His happiness came from making others happy around him. I noticed this about my father—how giving he was to others around him, and expecting absolutely nothing in return.

I shared this story with the student because it epitomizes what I believe is important in a leader—being someone that consistently gives, instead of just takes, from those around them.

It was nice to think of my father that day, and reminded me of how little moments of inspiration travel with you even through decades of life. I think of how my father shared the fish with others as one of my ideals in leader-behavior that I've always admired seeing when it happens. Sharing is caring, and I'm glad to share this thought with you.

Being the Answer, via George Clooney

First published online on 8 October 2011

Last week with the loss of Steve Jobs I'm a bit off balance like many out there. I shared some of my thoughts with NPR's Morning Edition, but am still way bummed right now. I clip a lot of things out of magazines and the likes and put them in my wallet, and rifling through it this morning I found something that gave me a needed smile. It's from an interview with actor George Clooney on the topic of failure from Parade Magazine.

> **You've talked about how lucky you are. What have you learned from your failures?**
>
> It's hard when you get thumped. I've been proficient at failure. But the only thing you can do is say, "Here's what I won't do next time."
>
> I was a baseball player in school. I had a good arm, I could catch anything, but I was having trouble hitting. I would be like, "I wonder if I'll hit it; just let me hit the ball." And then I went away for the fall, learned how to hit, and by my sophomore year I'd come to the plate and think, "I wonder where I want to hit the ball, to the left or right?" Just that little bit of skill and confidence changed everything. Well,

I had to treat acting like that. I had to stop going to auditions thinking, "Oh, I hope they like me." I had to go in thinking I was the answer to their problem. You could feel the difference in the room immediately.

The greatest lesson I learned was that sometimes you have to fake it. And you have to be willing to fail.

Thanks George. Thanks Steve.

Service-Minded and Hospitality-Minded

First published online on 28 January 2012

When I first arrived at RISD, I was given a book by our talented head of dining and retail, Ginnie Dunleavy, called *Setting the Table* about the concept of hospitality. I always enjoyed the basic thesis of the book— "Is the customer always right?" The answer is no—but, "They must always feel heard."

Four years later, I became suddenly compelled to read, *The Cornell School of Hotel Administration on Hospitality*—it makes a precise distinction between hospitality and service in a variety of ways. It reads:

> If hospitality is heavily qualitative, then service is more quantitative. Service can be scripted and dictated, mechanical, and drilled. You can evaluate service more easily than hospitality. Service is repetitive, efficient, consistent, continuous, tailored, customized, and sustainable. Unlike hospitality, service is much easier to perfect through training, drill, exercise, and continuous commitment. With such practice, service can be taken to the highest level of technical perfection. But for true excellence, service and hospitality must combine. One cannot exist without the other.

It goes on to describe hospitality as those qualities that relate to certain keywords like: *warmth, friendly, listening, respect, treatment, guest, sensitivity, genuine, memorable,* and *unique.*

As someone who grew up working in a small factory in Seattle and having had the privilege of serving many customers from dawn to dusk, six (and sometimes seven) days a week with my family, I never thought much about what made it a solvent business. Our product was priced lower than our competitors, and yet the quality was much higher. There were no employees besides my siblings and mom/dad, so you could say that labor costs were lower than normal. It didn't quite make sense to me.

My father believed in the quality of work as something vital to his being—as trained to be someone who makes things exquisitely well. So if he needed to sustain the quality of his product, *tofu,* at an absurdly high level, he would select the best soybean seeds and the best natural *ni-gari* that he could procure. And of course, he'd progressively reduce his margins in the process.

My mother didn't have a business background as well, and yet somehow their little business survived many ups and downs. And their overall "business" goal could be achieved—which was to send me and my siblings all off to college so that we might not have to make *tofu* for a living.

The Cornell book was useful because it gave me the *aha* I could not articulate for all these years. Dad was *service*—which was embodied in the product that he made to a high level of perfection. And mom was *hospitality*—which is the real reason that customers came back.

I recall countless arguments between my parents because my mother would often talk to customers at length—she was from Hawaii and with her inimitable charm could keep customers in our storefront forever. The arguments would be grounded in my father's silent need to silently make the product in the backroom, and to want her help in that process. Meanwhile in the storefront, because of my mom the customer has lingered for so long that they can't help but buy a few of the Japanese canned goods (with higher margins) on our shelves. And furthermore, the customer has personally committed to come back again to if at least chat with my radiant mom with her Hawaiian warmth as an antidote to the famous Seattle rainy weather.

The line above from the Cornell book says it all:

But for true excellence, service and hospitality must combine. One cannot exist without the other.

Luckily they stayed married all those years, and still are.

Wanting Your Way Gets In The Way

First published online on 1 August 2012

I recently attended a conference of 100 Internet-related innovators that was held at a private home in the Midwest. The couple who owned this venue were the kindest people one could imagine— opening up their entire home for a group of complete strangers to "unconference" in their living rooms and backyard for several days.

Every morning—this older couple, let's call them Irene and Harold—
would reservedly and excitedly speak into a microphone to share
their welcomes to launch each new day of activities. On the third day,
all the visitors were feeling fully comfortable in the surrounds, and
there was an exciting panel about to start with everyone buzzedly
gathering on the tented lawn. Irene picked up the microphone
looking uncharacteristically disappointed and without being able
to get everyone's focus and attention, spoke softly, "Excuse me. We
have signs on the doors of the house to ask you to kindly not bring
drinks and food into the house … can you … ." At which point the
event's organizer/emcee took the microphone from Irene and said
in a slightly louder voice, "Excuse me everyone." People immediately
took attention as this was coming from the organizer who arranged
the event—the one who got his longtime friends Irene and Harold to
co-host and cover all the costs for this gathering.

"Excuse me everyone," the organizer said sternly. And then
softened. "Who here thinks that our friends Irene and Harold have
been the most wonderful of hosts for all of us here?" We all naturally
raised our hands. "Good," he said smiling, "And now, who here feels
that Irene has greeted us every morning with kindness and grace
that has made you feel truly welcome in her home?" We all began
to cheer, and Irene broke out into a brilliant smile. He went on, "Who
here … will do anything for Irene to thank her and Harold for these
past few days?" The entire group applauded. "And who here thinks
that spilling drinks on Irene's carpet when all the doors have signs
that clearly read 'No drinks or food in the house, please.' runs counter
to honoring our hosts' simple request?" A resounding "YES" resulted.

"Let us now enjoy this panel, and thank you all for your attention. And thank you, again, Irene and Harold!"

The brilliance of the organizer's interjection, in my mind, was twofold:

1. The organizer made the co-hosts feel proud of their act of hospitality by recognizing them and honoring them broadly. Irene's request was couched within the overall respect the crowd owed to her—and was unfortunately starting to blissfully ignore their debt.

2. The organizer made the audience feel as though they were led to the natural conclusion of what "the right thing" was by grounding an act of compliance within the context of gratitude. We all owed Irene (and Harold) a debt of gratitude that could be partly repaid right there and then by simply following their one rule.

I thought how, in contrast, any other organizer might have grabbed the microphone from Irene and instead sternly admonished the entire crowd for spilling a drink inside the house even when signs were clearly posted everywhere—which would have soured the mood of the gathering because there was only one culprit hiding amongst us all, but the entire group would unnecessarily bear the message's negativity. And furthermore, it could only unjustifiably draw negative feelings towards Irene from those partygoers who can't stand a buzzkill (even when the buzz deserves to be killed).

I shared this story with a CEO friend who said it reminded him of Abraham Lincoln's famous speech that helped to move the civil war between the North and the South to an end by appealing to "the better angels in all of us." In other words, speaking to the sense of possibility and humanity that we all so easily forget when we're completely distracted by the events at hand—in this case the good times people can have at the expense of others and forget their manners.

How leaders enable—through simply pointing out what matters most within the medium of a moment of time and when getting everyone's attention is impossible—a group of complete strangers to unite and act as one continues to strike me as an enormously creative space in which to explore and learn.

My Four Rules

First published online on 21 November 2012

In 1999 I made these four rules for myself to live by. One of my Public Safety officers at RISD recalled me talking about them on campus three years ago and asked to be reminded what they were—and I had forgotten them, and couldn't find them on my old websites at MIT. Here they are, unearthed and a little bit dusty, thanks to the archaeology work of a close friend.

I can't remember what motivated my putting these down to paper—I recall that it was shortly after I became a professor at MIT and was trying to figure out this "leadership" thing. I still strive to live by these rules every day—failing more than succeeding, but I love to keep trying through doing and I don't intend to give up.

1. ***Don't speak ill of others.*** It's human nature to knock the other party down when they aren't watching as a natural survival instinct. I always admire the people I meet in life who never feel they have to speak ill of others to make themselves look good.

2. ***Avoid passive aggressive behavior.*** Failing to be forthright with what you really want to say can be hurtful. Being honest and respectful is a good way to deliver a difficult message.

3. *Listen broadly, but don't waffle on decisions.* When people depend upon you to make a decision, they're basically asking you to be responsible for the possible failed outcome. Your decision should be based upon expert opinions culled from your team, but in the end you make the final decision and are the one responsible—you bear the responsibility for the team. If you're wrong, admit you're wrong early and things will usually go better that way. If you're right then consider yourself lucky and pass on the win to your team. Keep moving forward.

4. *When in error—admit, apologize, move forward.* I am not perfect. The only way that I can guarantee not making any mistakes is if I were to do absolutely nothing. So by doing anything at all, I risk making errors of varying degree of intensity. When, and I will, make a mistake I will admit the error as soon as possible, apologize for it, and then move forward without being paralyzed.

Generosity as Doing, Not Thinking

First published online on 7 June 2013

My father never said much to me as I was growing up. He was a doer, more than a thinker. Because my father could only speak Japanese, many people thought I could speak Japanese too. Nope. I could understand a lot though, as he was often giving instructions on what I should do. So if I knew a few spoken words in Japanese as a youth in my "conversations" with my dad it was an obedient, "Yes. I'll do it."

There's one thing I learned from my father, by watching how he'd interact with everyone around him, that had nothing to do with language. Or about thinking. Just doing. And it was doing nice things for other people. He was always someone to go the extra mile for a friend. And he never asked for anything in return. This always struck me as odd—having observed the world outside of his sphere (ie "the real world") in comparison year over year growing up—wondering to myself, "What was dad's doing … giving everything he had … away?"

When we think of strategy, we usually think of managing scarcity. Or, choosing the best outcome among other alternatives. Dad never seemed to act from a position of "strategy" in his business, and in his dealings with non-business friends and people. He seemed fully comfortable giving away whatever he had, and just assuming he would always make more. Of what?

I now realize that he created massive amounts of generosity. If I may be more specific, he inspired me to believe that generosity was something that you *do*, and not something that you think about doing. Otherwise it isn't being generous at all.

Dad loved the confidence he embodied in himself—to be generous, for generosity's sake—with no particular reason why he *could* be generous at all. He was enigmatic in his ways. Instructive as a doer. Doing is a way of thinking out loud too. That sounds right. Now I get it … it's always helpful to think out loud.

Okay, my ten minute doing-as-blogging break is over … thanks for visiting.

Notes

Chapter 1

1 John Maeda interview, 7/10/23.

2 Howard University Vernon E. Jordan Law Library, "A Brief History of Civil Rights in the United States: Desegregation," last updated January 6, 2023, https://library.law.howard.edu/civilrightshistory/blackrights/desegregation.

3 John Maeda, "Star Trek and Dr. Martin Luther King Jr.", LinkedIn post, January 16, 2023, www.linkedin.com/pulse/star-trek-dr-martin-luther-king-jr-dr-john-maeda.

4 Clayborne Carson and David L. Lewis, "Martin Luther King, Jr.", *Britannica*, last updated April 19, 2024, www.britannica.com/biography/Martin-Luther-King-Jr.

5 Sharon Boswell and Lorraine McConaghy, "Lights Out, Seattle," *The Seattle Times*, November 3, 1996, https://special.seattletimes.com/o/special/centennial/november/lights_out.html.

6 Phil Dougherty, "Chinese Vice Premier Deng Xiaoping (or Teng Hsiao-ping) Arrives in Seattle for a Two-day Visit on February 3, 1979," HistoryLink, www.historylink.org/File/8588.

7 Starbucks, "Our Company," www.starbucks.com/about-us.

8 John Maeda interview, 5/1/23.

9 John Maeda interview, 7/10/23.

10 John Maeda interview, 7/10/23.

11 Mitchell Schnurman, "Once a Respected Leader, RadioShack Used to Matter a Lot," *The Dallas Morning News,* February 5, 2015, www.dallasnews.com/business/2015/02/05/schnurman-once-a-respected-leader-radioshack-used-to-matter-a-lot/

12 John Maeda interview, 7/10/23.

13 John Maeda interview, 9/11/23.

14 MIT Media Lab, "About the Lab," www.media.mit.edu/about/history.

15 John Maeda interview, 7/10/23.

16 John Maeda interview, 7/10/23.

17 John Maeda, "The South Face of the Mountain," *MIT Technology Review*, July 1, 1998, www.technologyreview.com/1998/07/01/41574/the-south-face-of-the-mountain.

18 John Maeda interview, 7/10/23.

19 John Maeda interview, 9/11/23.

20 John Maeda interview, 7/10/23.

21 Tina Essmaker, "John Maeda," *The Great Discontent,* April 8, 2014, https://thegreatdiscontent.com/interview/john-maeda.

22 Maeda, "The South Face of the Mountain."

23 John Maeda interview, 7/10/23.

24 Maeda, "The South Face of the Mountain."

25 Sasha Arden, "Resurrecting the Digital Past: Access to Artistic Content on CD-ROMs," Tate Collection Care Research Writings, 2022, www.tate.org.uk/research/collection-care-research/resurrecting-the-digital-past-access-to-artistic-content-on-cd-roms.

26 John Maeda interview, 7/10/23.

27 John Maeda, "My Journey Back to Digital Product Design," LinkedIn post, November 11, 2015, www.linkedin.com/pulse/my-journey-back-digital-product-design-john-maeda.

28 John Maeda interview, 7/10/23.

29 John Maeda interview, 7/10/23.

30 Artvee, "Muriel Cooper," https://artvee.com/artist/muriel-cooper.

Chapter 2

1 MIT Media Lab, "Who We Are + What We Do + Why We Do It," www.media.mit.edu/about/overview.

2 MIT Media Lab, "About the Building," www.media.mit.edu/about/about-the-building.

3 MIT, "Reports to the President 1995–1996," https://web.mit.edu/annualreports/pres96/index.html.

4 Elizabeth Resnick, "Reputations: John Maeda," Eye, 37 (10), 2000, www.eyemagazine.com/feature/article/reputations-john-maeda.

5 Liz Stinson, "How Computer Code Became a Modern Design Medium—an Oral History," Eye on Design, December 5, 2019, https://eyeondesign.aiga.org/how-an-mit-research-group-turned-computer-code-into-a-modern-design-medium.

6 John Maeda interview, 7/10/23.

7 Holly Willis, "2010 AIGA Medalist: John Maeda," AIGA, September 9, 2010, www.aiga.org/membership-community/aiga-awards/2010-aiga-medalist-john-maeda.

8 Stinson, "How Computer Code Became a Modern Design Medium—an Oral History."

9 Claudia Dreifus, "A Conversation With: John Maeda; When M.I.T. Artist Shouts, His 'Painting' Listens," The New York Times, July 27, 1999, www.nytimes.com/1999/07/27/science/a-conversation-with-john-maeda-when-mit-artist-shouts-his-painting-listens.html.

10 MIT News, "John Maeda named president of Rhode Island School of Design," December 21, 2007, https://news.mit.edu/2007/announcement-risd-1222.

11 John Maeda interview, 10/30/23.

12 Ben Fry, "History of Processing, as told by John Maeda," August 25, 2009, https://benfry.com/writing/archives/513.

13 John Maeda, "Maeda Policy as a Professor," https://acg.media.mit.edu/people/maeda/maedapolicy.pdf.

14 John Maeda, "John Maeda," MIT Media Laboratory, July 22, 2003, https://acg.media.mit.edu/people/maeda.

15 John Maeda interview, 5/1/23.

16 John Maeda interview, 5/1/23.

17 John Maeda, *Maeda @ Media*, Thames & Hudson, https://thamesandhudson.com/maeda-at-media-9780500282359.

18 Cooper Hewitt, "2001 National Design Awards Winners," www.cooperhewitt.org/national-design-awards/2001-national-design-awards-winners.

19 Christian Wagner, "Honorary Doctor of Engineering: John Maeda," Honorary Awards Ceremony 2022, City University of Hong Kong, www.cityu.edu.hk/system/files/2022-11/citation_e_Maeda.pdf.

20 John Maeda interview, 10/30/23.

21 John Maeda interview, 5/1/23.

22 John Maeda interview, 5/1/23.

23 Editorial Reviews, Barnes and Noble, https://valsec.barnesandnoble.com/w/the-laws-of-simplicity-john-maeda/1117030018?.

24 John Maeda interview, 9/25/23.

25 John Maeda interview, 9/25/23.

26 InterCommunication Center, "John Maeda: Post Digital," August 10–October 21, 2001, www.ntticc.or.jp/en/exhibitions/2001/exhibition-john-maeda-post-digital.

27 Fondation Cartier pour l'art contemporain, "Exhibition: John Maeda, nature + eye'm hungry," November 19, 2005 to February 19, 2006, www.fondationcartier.com/en/exhibitions/john-maeda-nature-eyem-hungry.

28 Riflemaker London, "John Maeda," www.riflemaker.org/JohnMaedahome.

29 John Maeda interview, 9/25/23.

30 "The 75 Most Influential People of the 21st Century," *Esquire*, September 16, 2008, www.esquire.com/news-politics/g82/most-influential-21st-century-1008.

31 John Maeda interview, 10/30/23.

Chapter 3

1 RISD, "History and Tradition," www.risd.edu/about/history-and-tradition.

2 Essmaker, "John Maeda," *The Great Discontent.*

3 John Maeda interview, 10/30/23.

4 Rachel Berger, "RISD's New President Is a Signal of Changing Priorities in Design," *Eye on Design*, April 14, 2022, https://eyeondesign.aiga.org/risds-new-president-is-a-signal-of-changing-priorities-in-design.

5 MIT, "John Maeda Named President of Rhode Island School of Design," *MIT News*, December 21, 2007, https://news.mit.edu/2007/announcement-risd-1222.

6 John Maeda interview, 5/1/23.

7 John Maeda interview, 9/25/23.

8 Ben Hyman, "Maeda Inaugurated as RISD's President," *The Brown Daily Herald*, September 14, 2008, www.browndailyherald.com/article/2008/09/maeda-inaugurated-as-risd-s-president.

9 John Maeda interview, 10/30/23.

10 Bill Van Siclen, "RISD's Rock Star," *The Providence Journal,* June 1, 2008, www.providencejournal.com/story/news/2008/06/01/20080601-risd-s-rock-star-ece/35357681007.

11 RISD, "John Maeda Moves On," January 2, 2014, www.risd.edu/news/stories/john-maeda moves.

12 John Maeda interview, 9/11/23.

13 John Maeda, "Makers like to Make, Not Lead," Creative Leadership, February 2, 2013, http://creativeleadership.com/cl/screen-shot-2013-02-02-at 10-50-09-am-png.html.

14 John Maeda interview, 5/1/23.

15 RISD, "History and Tradition."

16 John Maeda interview, 9/11/23.

17 John Maeda interview, 9/11/23.

18 Doug Lederman, "RISD Faculty Vote No Confidence," *Inside Higher Ed*, March 6, 2011, www.insidehighered.com/quicktakes/2011/03/07/risd-faculty-vote-no-confidence.

19 Tory Elmore, "RISD Students Speak Out on No Confidence Vote," *GoLocalProv News*, March 3, 2011, www.golocalprov.com/news/risd-president-comes-under-fire.

20 Paddy Johnson, "RISD's President John Maeda Responds to No-Confidence Vote," *Art F City*, March 11, 2011, http://artfcity.com/2011/03/11/risds-president-john-maeda-responds-to-no-confidence-vote.

21 John Maeda interview, 10/9/23.

22 John Maeda interview, 10/9/23.

23 RISD, "History and Tradition."

24 John Maeda interview, 10/9/23.

25 James R. Langevin CV, https://home.watson.brown.edu/sites/default/files/People/Senior%20Fellows/James%20R%20Langevin_CV.pdf.

26 "Reps. Bonamici and Shock Announce Bipartisan Congressional Steam Caucus" [Press release], February 14, 2013, http://bonamici.house.gov/media/press-releases/reps-bonamici-and-schock-announce-bipartisan-congressional-steam-caucus.

27 Tim Mikulski, "'Sesame Street' Moves Full STEAM Ahead," ARTS Blog, August 27, 2012, https://blog.americansforthearts.org/2019/05/15/sesame-street-moves-full-steam-ahead.

28 John Maeda interview, 10/9/23.

29 John Maeda interview, 9/11/23.

30 John Maeda interview, 10/9/23.

31 John Maeda interview, 10/9/23.

32 Edna W. Lawrence Nature Lab, https://naturelab.risd.edu.

33 Megan Wu, "Quirky, the Failure of Invention Crowdsourcing," HBS Digital Initiative, last modified February 2, 2017, https://d3.harvard.edu/platform-digit/submission/quirky-the-failure-of-invention-crowdsourcing.

34 John Maeda interview, 5/29/23.

35 John Maeda interview, 10/9/23.

36 John Maeda interview, 5/29/23.

37 Nancy Blaker et al., "The Height Leadership Advantage in Men and Women: Testing Evolutionary Psychology Predictions about the Perceptions of Tall Leaders," Group Processes & Intergroup Relations, 16(1) (2013): 17–27.

38 John Maeda interview, 5/29/23.

39 Megan Rose Dickey, "The World's 25 Best Design Schools*," Business Insider, November 24, 2012, www.businessinsider.com/the-worlds-25-best-design-schools-2012-11.

40 RISD, "John Maeda Moves On."

41 John Maeda interview, 10/30/23.

42 RISD, "John Maeda Moves On."

Chapter 4

1 RISD, "John Maeda Moves On."

2 John Maeda interview, 7/10/23.

3 Wagner, "Honorary Doctor of Engineering: John Maeda," Honorary Awards Ceremony 2022, City University of Hong Kong.

4 John Maeda interview, 7/10/23.

5 Katie MacDonald, "Venture Capital: 146 Sixth Street (Location of Ionics)," Innovation in Cambridge, 2012, https://historycambridge.org/innovation/Venture%20Capital.html.

6 John Maeda interview, 7/10/23.

7 John Maeda interview, 10/30/23.

8 John Maeda interview, 10/9/23.

9 Tumblr, "Congrats, you have an all male panel!", www.tumblr.com/allmalepanels.

10 John Maeda interview, 10/9/23.

11 John Maeda interview, 10/30/23.

12 John Maeda, *Design in Tech Reports*, https://designintech.report.

13 SXSW, "About SXSW," www.sxsw.com/about.

14 John Maeda, *Design in Tech Report 2015*, https://designintech.report/2015/03/15/design-in-tech-report-2015.

15 John Maeda interview, 10/9/23.

16 Lorraine K. Lee, "The Must-Read SlideShares of 2015," LinkedIn post, December 19, 2015, www.linkedin.com/pulse/must-read-slideshares-2015-lorraine-k-lee.

17 John Maeda, *Design in Tech Report 2016,* https://designintech.report/2016/03/13/design-in-tech-report-2016.

18 John Maeda, *Design in Tech Report 2017*, https://designintech.report/wp-content/uploads/2017/03/dit-2017-1-0-7-compressed.pdf.

19 John Maeda, *CX Report 2020*, https://designintech.report/wp-content/uploads/2020/03/cxreport-appendix-small.pdf.

20 Marc Andreessen, "Why Software is Eating the World," *The Wall Street Journal*, August 20, 2011, https://www.wsj.com/articles/SB10001424053111903480904576512250915629460. Andreessen is the co-founder of Netscape and an influential investor.

21 John Maeda, *CX Report 2021*, https://cx.report/2021-cx-report.

22 John Maeda, *ResilienceTech Report,* https://resiliencetech.report.

23 John Maeda, *Design in Tech Report 2023*, https://designintech.report/sxsw2023.

24 John Maeda, *Design in Tech Report 2024* presentation transcript, March 8, 2024.

25 John Maeda interview, 10/9/23.

26 John Maeda, Twitter post, June 7, 2009, https://twitter.com/johnmaeda/status/2057122807?s=20.

27 "30 Best John Maeda Quotes With Image," *BooKey*, www.bookey.app/quote-author/john-maeda.

28 "30 Best John Maeda Quotes With Image," *BooKey*.

29 John Maeda interview, 10/9/23.

30 Katharine Schwab, "John Maeda: 'In Reality, Design is not that Important'," *Fast Company*, March 15, 2019, www.fastcompany.com/90320120/john-maeda-in-reality-design-is-not-that-important.

31 John Maeda interview, 10/30/23.

32 Elise Hu, "John Maeda on How Leaders Will Use AI to Unleash Creativity," *WorkLab,* April 19, 2023, www.microsoft.com/en-us/worklab/podcast/how-leaders-will-use-ai-to-unleash-creativity.

Chapter 5

1 John Maeda, "Why I Decided to Join a Technology Startup," LinkedIn post, August 18, 2016, www.linkedin.com/pulse/why-i-decided-join-technology-startup-john-maeda.

2 John Maeda interview, 12/11/23.

3 John Maeda, "2018 Automattic Design Award Winners Announced," *Automattic.Design*, December 11, 2018, https://automattic.design/2018/12/11/2018-automattic-design-award-winners-announced.

4 John Maeda, *Design in Tech Report 2018,* https://johnmaeda.github.io/#1.

5 Margaret Rhodes, "John Maeda: How a Fall Opened a New Chapter of Identity and Inclusion," Behance Blog, August 23, 2018, www.behance.net/blog/john-maeda-how-a-fall-opened-a-new-chapter-of-identity-and-inclusion.

6 John Maeda interview, 9/11/23.

7 John Maeda interview, 10/9/23.

 8 Editorial Reviews, Amazon, www.amazon.com/How-Speak-Machine-Computational-Thinking/dp/039956442X.

 9 Editorial Reviews, Barnes and Noble, https://valsec.barnesandnoble.com/w/how-to-speak-machine-john-maeda/1133016796.

10 John Maeda interview, 7/10/23.

11 John Maeda, "John Maeda | On Joining Publicis Sapient," YouTube video, June 19, 2019, https://youtu.be/eok1V2CXG8w.

12 Saron Yitbarek, "Why You Should Learn to Speak Machine with John Maeda," *CodeNewbie*, November 4, 2019, www.codenewbie.org/podcast/combining-art-and-tech-and-why-you-should-learn-to-speak-machine.

13 John Maeda interview, 10/30/23.

14 John Maeda, "How Can We #MakeRoom for the Next Generation of Leaders?", LinkedIn post, September 24, 2020, www.linkedin.com/pulse/how-can-we-makeroom-next-generation-leaders-dr-john-maeda.

15 NFL Football Operations, "The Rooney Rule," https://operations.nfl.com/inside-football-ops/inclusion/the-rooney-rule.

16 Maeda, "How Can We #MakeRoom for the Next Generation of Leaders?"

17 Everbridge, "Everbridge insights with John Maeda," February 12, 2021, www.everbridge.com/customers/success-center/resource/everbridge-insights-with-john-maeda.

18 Everbridge, "Everbridge Appoints World-renowned Technologist, and 'One of the Most Influential People of the 21st Century,' as Chief Customer Experience Officer to Innovate the Next Generation of Critical Event Management (CEM)," October 12, 2020, https://ir.everbridge.com/news-releases/news-release-details/everbridge-appoints-world-renowned-technologist-and-one-most.

19 Everbridge, "Everbridge Appoints World-renowned Technologist, and 'One of the Most Influential People of the 21st Century,' as Chief Customer Experience Officer to Innovate the Next Generation of Critical Event Management (CEM)."

20 John Maeda, "Safety Eats The World: Why I Joined Everbridge," LinkedIn post, October 15, 2020, www.linkedin.com/pulse/safety-eats-world-why-i-joined-everbridge-dr-john-maeda.

21 Everbridge, "COVID-19 R2R Autumn 2020," https://go.everbridge.com/covid-19-road-to-recovery-autumn-symposium.html.

22 Everbridge, "Recognizing the Importance of Critical Event Management (CEM) Amid COVID-19, Everbridge's Dr. John Maeda Ranked 11th on LinkedIn's 2020 Top Influencer List," December 7, 2020, https://ir.everbridge.com/news-releases/news-release-details/recognizing-importance-critical-event-management-cem-amid-covid.

23 Everbridge, "Everbridge Chief Experience Officer Dr. John Maeda Presents on the Critical Role of Software in Creating a Safer World at 2021 SXSW Global Conference," March 10, 2021, www.everbridge.com/newsroom/article/everbridge-chief-experience-officer-dr-john-maeda-presents-on-the-critical-role-of-software-in-creating-a-safer-world-at-2021-sxsw-global-conference.

24 John Maeda interview, 12/11/23.

25 John Maeda, "THE BLUEST SKIES," LinkedIn post, November 2022, www.linkedin.com/posts/johnmaeda_the-bluest-skies-i-grew-up-hearing-the-perry-activity-6995827178911191040-o5E9.

26 John Maeda interview, 12/11/23.

27 John Maeda, "THE BLUEST SKIES."

28 John Maeda, *Design in Tech Report 2024*, https://designintech.report.

29 Associated Press, "Programmer and Inventor of the ELIZA Computer Language," *Los Angeles Times*, March 14, 2008, www.latimes.com/archives/la-xpm-2008-mar-14-me-weizenbaum14-story.html.

30 Joseph Weizenbaum, *Computer Power and Human Reason: From Judgment to Calculation* (San Francisco: W. H. Freeman, 1976) quoted in John Maeda, "Joseph Weizenbaum," December 29, 2019, https://maeda.pm/2019/12/29/joseph-weizenbaum.

31 John Maeda interview, 9/25/23.

32 John Maeda interview, 9/25/23.

33 Madagascar Spices Company, "Madagascar Cacao," www. madagascarspices.com/cacao.html.

34 John Maeda interview, 9/25/23.

35 Microsoft Developer, "Mr. Maeda's Cozy AI Kitchen," YouTube channel, www.youtube.com/playlist?list=PLIrxD0HtieHjHoXHYSiSvpTp_sE5JhNEE.

36 John Maeda interview, 10/9/23.

37 Microsoft Developer, "Mr. Maeda's Cozy AI Kitchen: Secure Insights with Tracy Reinhold," YouTube video, January 10, 2024, www.youtube.com/ watch?v=-w7J7jXg-CA&ab_channel=MicrosoftDeveloper.

38 John Maeda interview, 5/29/23.

39 John Maeda interview, 5/29/23.

40 John Maeda, "THE BLUEST SKIES."

41 John Maeda interview, 5/29/23.

42 City University of Hong Kong, "Two distinguished persons conferred honorary doctorates at CityU," CityUHK Updates, December 2022, www. cityu.edu.hk/cityupdate/media/news/2022/11/04/two-distinguished-persons-conferred-honorary-doctorates-cityu.

43 Kahlil Gibran, "On Joy and Sorrow," https://poets.org/poem/joy-and-sorrow.

44 John Maeda interview, 12/11/23.